Strangers on a Train

A play

Craig Warner

Based on the novel by Patricia Highsmith

Samuel French — London
New York - Toronto - Hollywood

STRANGERS ON A TRAIN

First produced at the Gateway Theatre, Chester, on 29th
March 1996 with the following cast of characters:

Charles Bruno	Dominic McHale
Guy Haines	Gerard Logan
Elsie Bruno	Naomi Buch
Anne Faulkner	Jade Taylor
Frank Myers	Blair Plant
Robert Treacher	Jason O'Mara
Arthur Gerard	Chris Johnston

Directed by Madeleine Wynn

It was subsequently produced at the Mercury Theatre,
Colchester, on 31st August 2000 with the following cast
of characters:

Charles Bruno	Alan Cox
Guy Haines	Stephen Billington
Elsie Bruno	Diane Fletcher
Anne Faulkner	Alexandra Staden
Frank Myers	Stephen Ballantyne
Robert Treacher	William Oxborrow
Arthur Gerard	Michael Elwyn

Directed by Ian Brown
Designed by Peter McKintosh

CHARACTERS

Charles Bruno
Guy Haines
Elsie Bruno
Anne Faulkner
Frank Myers
Robert Treacher
Arthur Gerard

The action takes place in America

Time—1950s

AUTHOR'S NOTE

In designing a set for this play, the intention was to create several spaces, each of which could be used for several scenes:

- UR, on an elevated platform, a bedroom, which serves as the room at the Hotel La Fonda and also Bruno's bedroom at home
- DR, a table and chairs, which serve as the dining-car on the train, the New York bar, and Guy's office
- C, a small room with a couch or cot which serves as Guy's apartment, with a curtain upstage leading to the kitchen
- DL, a sitting-room, which serves as both the villa in Mexico and later as the Haines's living-room
- UL, a staircase leading up to Bruno's father's room
- somewhere, a public phone

There are other arrangements which would be just as effective. With so many locations it seems important to keep the set simple so that the audience's imagination, rather than physical properties, can fill in the details. That said, designers might try to make some of the scenes — those in the Haines's living-room, for instance — warm and homey and real. It is not a world of shadows. It is an everyday world — a cosy, protected world — which is slowly invaded by desolation.

Finally, though the demands of the stage and duties as an author have led me to change some elements of the story, I tried always to write within the spirit of the original novel. For research and inspiration, there can be no substitute for reading the source material, Patricia Highsmith's great book, *Strangers on a Train*.

ACT I

SCENE 1

The dining-car of a train

Guy is at a table, reading a book, an empty glass in front of him. Other than that, the car is empty

Bruno appears at one end of the aisle and slowly walks along it. He stops near Guy and stares out the window. He finishes what's in his glass, and fills it from a silver hip flask he has in his pocket. He half-turns to Guy

Bruno You want a drink?

Guy I've got one here.

Bruno I find alcohol enhances travelling. What are you reading?

Guy Plato.

Bruno Wow!

Guy I just grabbed it off the shelf on my way out the door. I didn't think I'd actually read it.

Bruno I never read. I'd rather live the story than read about it. No offence to people who read! I'm sure some people read *and* live, and I'll bet you're one of them.

Guy What makes you so sure?

Bruno You've got a spark. I can spot a spark a mile off.

Guy laughs. Bruno sits

(*Offering the flask*) Here. Have a drink.

Guy No, really.

Bruno Do you like the flask? My mother gave it to me when I turned eighteen. It's got grapes and apples engraved on it. I understand the grapes — they mean wine, but I don't know why the apples are there. Do you?

Guy No.

Bruno Maybe for everything you understand there should be something else you don't. (*He drinks*) My name is Charles Bruno.

Guy Guy Haines.

Bruno There. We've introduced ourselves. Now we're not strangers. You can drink with me now.

Bruno sets the flask on the table and slides it over to Guy. Guy hesitates, then pours Scotch into his glass

Where are you going?
Guy Metcalf, Texas.
Bruno On business?

Guy says nothing

You can trust me. You'll never see me again. You can say anything you like.
Guy Where are you going?
Bruno Santa Fe.
Guy What's in Santa Fe?
Bruno Nothing really. Sometimes I go to a place just because I've never been there before. Don't you ever do that?
Guy No.
Bruno You like to stay at home.
Guy Yeah.
Bruno With your book.
Guy Yeah.
Bruno What does it say?
Guy You want me to read it to you?
Bruno Yeah.
Guy Here?
Bruno There's nobody else around. Just pick up where you left off.
Guy (*reading*) "The human soul can be likened to a pair of horses, one white, one black, each pulling their driver toward a different path. The white horse is good, the black, base; and the driver, through his days on earth, labours ever to steer the two horses on a single road."
Bruno I've said it all my life: every man's got a god and a murderer inside him, and either one of those can get let out at any time if life plays him right.
Guy I don't have a murderer in me.
Bruno You do!
Guy I can't swat a fly. It's not in my nature.
Bruno It's nothing to do with nature, every man's got them both, the good and the bad, the black horse and the white horse, your nature's just what's there on the surface! But that's what's great about being a human being, isn't it? All that stuff inside us, so much we can be capable of, and guilty of, and feel and do on this earth? I think we start out without any limits, immortal, dark black, blinding white, and as soon as we land on this earth we start to shrivel up and forget our true colours and become small and mortal and grey. Grey horses! I think that's probably the worst thing that happens to us on this earth. Don't you?

Guy (*quietly*) I do. I probably do.

Bruno What are you thinking?

Guy Aw, nothing, I ——

Bruno Tell me.

Guy I have a gun.

Bruno You have a gun!

Guy (*laughing*) Not here! At home, in a drawer. I bought it when I was fifteen with the money from my paper route. It's a little silver revolver with a short barrel and a pearl handle.

Bruno You have a gun.

Guy I never thought of it as something that could kill. I just bought it because it was beautiful.

Bruno And you've never fired it?

Guy No.

Bruno You've got to fire it!

Guy It's never been fired. That's part of its beauty.

Bruno It's a gun. It's got to be fired!

Guy What should I fire at?

Bruno That's something you'll have to figure out for yourself.

Guy laughs

You want to come to Santa Fe with me?

Guy I can't.

Bruno I've got plenty of money. I've got nothing to do till my mother gets there. You could be my guest. We could have a wild time!

Guy I've got things to do.

Bruno Like what?

Guy After I leave Metcalf I've got three days in Mexico. Then I've got to go to Palm Beach to start a job.

Bruno What kind of job?

Guy I'm building a country club.

Bruno You're an architect!

Guy Yeah.

Bruno A whole country club at your age!

Guy It might not work out.

Bruno Why not?

Guy Something's in the way.

Bruno What is? What is?

Silence

Aw, you can tell me, Guy! I'm just a stranger on the train, remember? You can say anything you like.

Silence

What's it going to be called?
Guy The Palmyra.
Bruno I'm going to join the Palmyra.
Guy Yeah?
Bruno Right now! Give me your glass! (*He pours*) To the Palmyra's first member, Charles Bruno. Clink my glass and I'll know I'm it!

Guy clinks his glass

Whooooeeeeee! You're going to be famous! We've got to do things in this life! I want to be immortal, I want to leave a trail of amazing deeds behind me, things no-one'll ever forget! So much is going to happen, I know it is, but for now I'm just waiting, waiting ...
Guy For what?
Bruno To live my life! My income was supposed to start this year, but my father won't let me have it. He's sending all my money into his own exchequer so I don't have any more cash now than I had when I was at school.
Guy You seem to do OK.
Bruno Yeah, but it's not OK because all the pleasures get dirty coming through his hands. It's not even his money, it belongs to my mother's family! He had his name put on it when I was a kid!
Guy Why'd he do that?
Bruno He robs whoever he can! Now he says he won't give me my money because I won't work for him, but that's a lie. He's just jealous because my mom and I have such a good time. Well I don't see why a person should work if they don't have to. In my opinion, all business is legalized throat-cutting, just like marriage is legalized fornication. Am I right?

Guy laughs

And to top it all off, he plays little games with me — like sometimes when I want to go out, he locks up my car in the garage and he won't give me the keys, for no reason at all, just to keep me from having a life! He never goes out, so everybody else has to stay in too. Can you think of anything worse than that? *It makes me sick!* I tell you, it's always been their mission, the mediocre, grey horse people, to smother anyone who's got a hint of a spark in them, hasn't it? *Why?* Because they can't *be* us, so they want to *kill* us. But they can't kill us, because they can't kill, they can't know their black horse, they're grey and grey forever, so the best they can do is to try to make us grey too! Well it's not going to work. When my dad is dead, and I promise you that can't be soon enough for me, I'm going to live. And when I die ... Well ... (*He looks out the window*) I'm never going to die.

Bruno turns to look at Guy and their eyes meet. They watch each other for a moment

Come to Santa Fe with me.
Guy How can I do that?
Bruno Just stay on the train.
Guy I've got to go to Metcalf.
Bruno Why? You're not building something there too?
Guy Tearing something down. I'm arranging my divorce.
Bruno You're married?

Beat

Was she unfaithful?

Pause

I can tell by your silence she was. What kind of girl was she? One of those dumb southern redheads with a little-girl voice who gets married young and then finds she gets easily bored?
Guy You don't aim wide of the mark, do you?
Bruno I know that kind of woman. My father had a string of them, a string of ... what's her name?
Guy Miriam.
Bruno A string of Miriams and so I know the kind of girl you mean. I know the way they smile and the way they laugh, the way they keep catching sight of themselves in the mirror, how they look when they accept a gift, how they lie underneath you like machines. I know Miriam. I know her inside and out.

Guy pours himself another Scotch

Are you going to tell me what happened?

Silence

Tell me anything you want, Guy. We don't know each other. We've never even met.
Guy My best friend Lawrence. Ha! That's what happened. My best friend Lawrence happened. I can see them together without even closing my eyes,

I just think of it and the image appears in front of me, the daylight in Chicago, stripes of light from the slats of the window on her back, where her shoes are, I still remember, all framed in the doorway like a photograph, with its own colours and sounds and smells, like a horrible little work of art. I was pulled to pieces, and worse again when I got the news that it had been going on all along, and not just with Lawrence, and that everybody knew.

Bruno And you're still married to her.

Guy I didn't need to think about a divorce until now.

Bruno What's changed?

Guy She's going to have a child.

Bruno Not yours.

Guy Not mine. And you want to know the joke?

Bruno What?

Guy She wants to come to Palm Beach with me while I build the Palmyra.

Bruno Why?

Guy Because the father of her child is married and he won't be free till September.

Bruno She's going to soil the whole thing with her filthy little hands.

Guy She says if I don't take her, she's going to come anyway.

Bruno She can't build, so she has to destroy.

Guy But her powers only extend so far. If she won't see reason, I'm going to turn down the job.

Bruno She's not going to see reason.

Guy That's why I'm not getting my hopes up about doing the Palmyra.

Bruno You can't let her lose you the chance of a lifetime!

Guy What am I going to do? Making a building is a spiritual act. I can't do it with her there. I won't. Oh hell, another job like this might crop up. She's not going to see reason.

Bruno Why should she? She's not a reasonable thing. She's just a thing to be stopped.

Guy How?

Bruno You don't think you have a killer inside you? Well you should find him — and start with her.

Guy Not me!

Bruno I'll do it then, with pleasure! It would be so easy! She's not a person, she's just a thing to be stopped, just a warm thing somewhere that needs to get put out. I'll tell you what: I'll kill her for you if you kill my father for me. Is that a deal?

Guy (*laughing*) Sure!

Bruno Think about it! We swap murders, then nobody could find us, because none of the clues would make any sense! There would be no motive, we'd have alibis — you wouldn't even know when I was going to do it!

Suddenly, out of the blue, it would be done, you'd be free, and nobody'd come looking for me because we're strangers, we haven't even met! What do you think, Guy? Clink my glass on it! Come on! It would be the perfect pair of murders, it would drive the cops crazy, it would be worth it just for that, even if we didn't *know* the people we were killing, but since without these two people we're free, Guy, all the white horses and black horses in heaven and hell and everywhere in between would be stampeding by our side! Clink my glass! *Clink it!*

Guy (*laughing*) To the power and elegance of your imagination, Bruno. (*He clinks his glass*)

Bruno Charley. Please call me Charley.

The Lights cross-fade to the next scene

SCENE 2

A hotel room, where Elsie Bruno puts on make-up at the vanity and talks to a closed bathroom door

Elsie Five minutes. You've got five minutes before I open that door and drag you out, and if I smell whisky I'm going to give you a hiding, I don't care how old you are. You're still my boy. Charley? Five minutes.

Pause

Look at my face. The light around here might as well be an X-ray. I could see myself, just then, as an old woman. For a split second she was there, staring back at me, but now she's gone again. Not a million miles away, but gone for now.

Pause

It's you that keeps me young, Charley. You're still my best friend. Hurry up and we'll go shopping. There's a silver belt I wanted to get which is two hundred and fifty dollars, now you tell me what to do, you always give such good advice — should I get it myself, or should I get Fred Wiley to buy it for me? There's no point coming to Santa Fe if you don't walk away with some silver clanking about on your person, and Fred Wiley's an easy target because unless I give him a chance to give me a goodbye present he might want to follow me to California, and that could cause problems it would be wise to prevent! You never know, though; it might be fun. "Chips fall where they may", as your father is fond of saying. "They might fall at your feet."

Pause

Then again, they might not.

Pause

They all swear their eternal love to me, Charley. Do you know they all still
swear to your old mother their eternal love.

*Bruno opens the bathroom door and stands there, wearing pyjama
bottoms and a dinner-jacket, a glass of Scotch in his hand*

Bruno That's because you've got the best legs of any woman of any age in
the world. Ziegfeld thought so, and he should know! (*He downs the Scotch*)
Elsie Charley! How many drinks this morning?
Bruno Just one.
Elsie (*approaching and sniffing*) I smell two.
Bruno OK two! I feel better since I drink a little more, Ma. Scotch opens the
blood vessels.
Elsie Then your blood vessels must be like garden hoses!

He grabs her

Bruno Dance with me!
Elsie *Charley!*
Bruno Tell me you'll be my Valentine.
Elsie It's only June!
Bruno Tell me anyway!
Elsie I've always been your Valentine.
Bruno And not the captain's.
Elsie Can't you say Daddy like most people?
Bruno Tell me!
Elsie You're my two best boys.

Bruno pulls away from her

Bruno Your face is never lit up when he's in the room.
Elsie That's 'cause when he's in the room I have to be a grown-up, you know
that, honey. And when we're alone, you and me ——
Bruno There's no parents!
Elsie That's right, baby!

Bruno picks up the Plato book

Bruno You know, in this book it says we've got black horses and white
horses in all of us, but I don't think it's true of you and Dad.
Elsie No?
Bruno I think you're all the good for both of you, and he's all the bad.
Everything clean and beautiful and good is on your side, and everything
useless and filthy and ——
Elsie Charley!
Bruno Ugly ——
Elsie Don't say things like that about your father! (*She snatches the book
from him*) And when did you start reading books?
Bruno I found it on the train.

Elsie opens the book

Elsie (*reading inside the cover*) Well you better mail it back to Mr Guy
Haines as soon as you can because it'll take at least two days to get to
Metcalf and he'll think he's lost it for good!
Bruno He'll get it back.
Elsie Oh Charley, come to California!
Bruno I have things to do!
Elsie You're meeting a woman, aren't you!
Bruno No!
Elsie You wouldn't lie to me?
Bruno Never!
Elsie Because you know I'm the only woman who'll ever understand you.
Bruno I know.
Elsie I'm the only woman who'll ever really love you!
Bruno Most women aren't worth the powder on their faces.
Elsie Promise you'll come to California as soon as you can?
Bruno Two days. I promise.
Elsie OK. I'll wait for you downstairs. And no sneaky drinks!
Bruno (*using the Plato book as a Bible*) I swear, Mom!

Elsie leaves the room

Bruno takes a swig from his hip flask and dials the phone

Train station, please ... Can you book one ticket for the four o'clock train
to Metcalf, Texas, in the name of Charles Bruno? I'll pay for it when I get
there. Thank you.

Bruno hangs up and goes into the bathroom, shutting the door behind him

The Lights cross-fade to the next scene

SCENE 3

A villa in Mexico

Anne screams, off, and runs in, laughing. Guy chases her on. She is half-dressed

Anne No honey, my dad's coming — stop it now!

He grabs her and kisses her neck

Guy He knows what men and women do when they're left alone together.
Anne He doesn't think we do those things! He's old-fashioned!

Guy persists in his lovemaking. Anne cautiously enjoys it

Anne I heard a noise.
Guy I didn't.

He persists. She gently tries to disentangle herself from him

Anne He'll be here any minute and the window's just there and he thinks we've got separate villas down here and he doesn't even know we spend the night together sometimes in that dingy little room of yours in New York and — Guy, you're still married!

Guy lets her go

Guy We promised each other when we crossed the border into Mexico we weren't going to mention Miriam once the whole weekend.
Anne I didn't mention her. (*She turns her back to him*) Here. Do me up.
Guy (*zipping up her dress*) I just wanted three days without her. She follows me wherever I go!
Anne (*turning*) Oh now don't be silly. Little kisses. Forehead.

He kisses her forehead

Elbow.

He kisses her elbow

Nose.

He kisses her nose

Finger.

He kisses her finger

Lips.

They kiss

Guy I wonder if I'll ever feel about you the way I feel about her now.

Anne looks up at him, shocked

I don't know why I said that. I'm furious about the Palmyra. I can't get her out of my head!

Anne You have a choice, Guy.

Guy She's insisting on coming! She says she's going to come whether I like it or not!

Anne So? Couldn't you just put up with her for a while? You put up with her all these years ...

Guy And I'm not putting up with her any more.

Anne You're crazy to let her run your life.

Guy She's not going to disgrace us in Palm Beach, Anne.

Anne She can't disgrace me.

Guy She can disgrace me.

Anne She can only disgrace herself.

Guy When I build, I need to get in touch with something higher inside me. Miriam blocks it off, she stands between me and whatever that thing is that lets me create. I couldn't work with her there.

Anne They'll steal your ideas.

Guy Don't rub it in!

Anne The louvre windows ...

Guy I know!

Anne Sweetie, I'm happy as long as you promise you won't regret it.

He holds her

Guy I won't regret it. This is just how things have turned out today. Who knows what may come our way tomorrow? Who knows what I might build? This is only one job, Anne. I have the rest of my life, with you, and that's all I need to know. And one day I'm going to build a bridge, a white bridge, it'll be all white, from one end to the other, with white arcs and white beams and white stone, white everything — like a bridge made out of light.

That'll be my wedding present to you ... But I have to give it to you now in the form of a promise.

They kiss

Anne A promise will do.

They kiss again

   Your credit is good here.

The phone begins to ring. He kisses her neck

   Guy, I can't reach the — sweetie ——

She laughs. He exposes her shoulder and kisses it

   Let me get the phone!

He lifts her

   Ahhh!

He brings her over to the table where the phone is ringing and seats her on it, starts to kiss her knees and her thighs

Anne (*laughing, whispering*) Guy, stop it! (*She lifts the receiver and tries to maintain composure*) Hallo? ... (*With emphasis as a signal for Guy to stop*) Hi, *Daddy*.

Guy insistently kisses his way up her thighs

   You're supposed to be here by now. We've got salads and Sangria coming in from room service. ... What? Say that again, Daddy, I'm having trouble with the ... Who?

What she hears now freezes her. Anne's eyes fill with tears as she listens. She slowly lowers the phone. Guy watches her eyes

   Guy, honey, I'm sorry. Somebody's murdered your wife.

She reaches out to him and touches his cheek. The Lights cross-fade to the next scene

Scene 4

A New York bar

The Lights come up dimly on a table DR

Bruno comes toward the table with two drinks, puts them down on the table, and sits. There are two places where Guy could sit: next to Bruno, diagonally, or at the other side of the table. Seated with his own drink, Bruno puts Guy's drink next to him. He then reconsiders and moves it across the table. He drinks. He brings the drink back to the diagonal position. He glances at his watch, looks around, tries to look relaxed

Guy enters wearing expensive new clothes and carrying an alligator briefcase. He sees Bruno, lingers a moment, then moves toward him

Bruno What a nice suit. How nice you look! And an alligator briefcase, that's very beautiful, Guy.

Guy I don't know why I'm here.

Bruno Sit down.

Guy What are you doing in New York?

Bruno I live here, Guy. I live in Great Neck. I don't travel all the time! Please sit.

Guy sits opposite Bruno

Guy Why did you want to see me so badly?

Bruno (*sliding the drink across the table to Guy*) I wanted a drink with the man who built the Palmyra. That's fair, isn't it? Here's a drink for you. A Scotch. I know you like Scotch once you settle into yourself.

Silence. Guy toys with his drink but does not drink it

You've got the glow of success. I take pride in that. I've seen pictures of you laying stones at the Palmyra and I've taken more pride in that than in anything else I've ever done.

Guy What the hell's it got to do with you?

Bruno (*taking out an initialled tie*) Here. I bought you a tie. You will wear it, won't you? It's got your initials on it.

Guy doesn't pick up the tie

You're not angry with me, are you? Come on, Guy. I did it for you.

Guy Did what?

Bruno She has a high laugh, doesn't she?
Guy You're insane.
Bruno You don't believe it was me, do you?
Guy If I did, I wouldn't be here.
Bruno Did you tell anyone you were coming to meet me?
Guy No.
Bruno Why not? If you didn't want to keep it a secret, why didn't you tell
anyone you were coming to meet me?
Guy Who should I tell? What should I say? Some lunatic keeps calling me
up ——
Bruno Guy, please ——
Guy I told myself if you called again I'd go to the police and tell them
everything.
Bruno But you didn't.
Guy No.
Bruno Why not?
Guy I don't know.
Bruno Because we're in it together.

Silence

You don't believe me, do you? You don't believe I did it. (*He downs half
his drink*) She's got red hair. She's quite pretty. A bit on the plump side,
but she's young, so it looks good.
Guy I described her on the train.
Bruno Did you? (*He swills the rest of his drink*) Twelve thirty-five Magnolia
Street. Is that where she lives? Near the junction of College Road? Maybe
it wasn't her. But on the night your wife was killed a red-haired girl came
out of twelve thirty-five Magnolia Street with a tall, skinny red-haired
brother laughing and talking in that little-girl voice they all use on their
daddies. They got in a green Chevy with another couple and drove out on
to a street called Crockett Boulevard. I followed them in a taxi. Twice we
lost the Chevy, and twice we found it again. We passed roadstands and
drive-in movies, and lots and lots of just plain old dark night till I thought
Crockett Boulevard must cross the whole state of Texas. And then the
Chevy pulled into a parking lot under a giant rainbow of lights, which said,
"Lake Metcalf's Kingdom of Fun".

Bruno suppresses a laugh

I followed them in. They all bought frozen custards. They went on the
merry-go-round. She got on a giraffe. She's covered with freckles. When
it stopped they got on a rowboat, and I got in another one, behind them. We

drifted around for a long time. They just wanted to float. But they ended up at the island, and they got off to stretch their legs. I was down the shore a piece from them. The other three sat down but I could hear her say she wouldn't sit because the ground was wet. She went for a walk. She walked straight toward me. She disappeared behind a rock but I could tell she was nearby because I could smell her perfume. I went behind the rock and I was so close to her I could feel the warmth of her body and I said, "Haven't I met you somewhere before?" She was a warm ugly black spot. She started to laugh. I threw my hands up at her throat and my body went hard like a rock and I could hear my tooth crack from the force and I cut off her laugh and held her throat too tight for her to scream and I put a leg behind her and pushed her back and we fell on to the ground together without making a sound, just a brush of leaves. I didn't like her underneath me but it kept her from getting away, and her throat got hotter and fatter and I had to push all my will into my fingers until her head stopped turning. I knew I'd held her long enough but I held her for a long time after, just to be sure. Then I let go and she made a sound like a cough and I had to press again, but I climbed on to my knees this time, right on top of her, and all the power in me was pouring through my hands. Then something in her ... *cracked*. And I knew I was done. I heard the other girl say, "Miriam", near the shore so I ran to my boat and I crossed the water and got away.

Bruno eases back into his chair

And you know what I was thinking? People are always talking about the wonder of birth, of a new life coming into the world, but nobody ever talks about the wonder of death. Where's Miriam now? I was with her, then I was alone. I took the life out of her body myself, by holding her throat too tight. Surely that's as much a miracle as birth.

Bruno tries to drink from his glass, but there is nothing in it

By the way, I think she was lying. She didn't look pregnant to me.

Guy chokes on a sob, but controls himself

Guy I hope you never stop suffering for what you've done.
Bruno What *we've* done, not me alone!
Guy I'm not in this with you, Bruno ...
Bruno You *asked* me to do it!
Guy I never asked!
Bruno You said it would be perfect, the perfect pair of murders ——
Guy *You* said that, not me!

Bruno You agreed! You agreed with me on the train!

Guy I never agreed to this. I'm leaving now.

Bruno No, Guy, please don't go! I'll tell if you go!

Guy What?

Bruno If you go, I'll tell everyone about our plan!

Guy What plan? We had no plan!

Bruno How's it going to look, Guy? Why would I kill your wife? I didn't even know her, why would I go to Metcalf to kill someone I don't even know?

Guy Don't try to contact me again.

Bruno You've got to finish it, Guy. I've given you your freedom, now you've got to give me mine!

Guy You're a lunatic, we haven't even met!

Bruno We have, Guy, and I want you to stick to the plan. I want you to kill my father.

Guy (*standing*) Don't ask to see me again, don't call ——

Bruno Don't leave!

Guy — or I swear I'll call the police!

Bruno Call them now, Guy.

Bruno waits

I said call them now. No? Why not?

Guy You just test me. If you don't stay out of my way ——

Bruno And keep silent? You want my silence, Guy?

Guy That's not what I said!

Bruno 'Cause you'll have to earn that.

Guy *What?!*

Bruno You have a motive, I don't. You know how they think. And I could look an angel in front of a jury. In fact, if you don't kill my father, I'll go to the police myself. I'll say you paid me to kill your wife. Come on, Guy, how's it going to look? My word against yours? You've got to come into it with me, you're not leaving me out here alone …

Guy You are alone.

Bruno stands and faces him

Bruno No Guy, you're with me in this, if only for one simple fact: That this deed I've done is like a crown on my head. And nobody can see it but you.

Guy stares at him, then walks off, leaving him alone

Bruno downs Guy's drink. The Lights cross-fade to the next scene

Scene 5

The Haines's living-room

The room is newly built but unfinished

*Myers appears in the frame of the front door wearing shabby work clothes.
He looks around, comes inside, and inspects the room with curiosity*

Anne backs into the room, shouting off into the kitchen

Anne I've had just about enough of this! Why don't we communicate by
letter? Then you won't have to hear the sound of my voice! (*She hasn't
noticed Myers, and nearly starts to cry*)

Myers Is it a bad time?

Anne Frank!

Myers The house is looking great.

Anne It's got a long way to go yet. I'm sorry about that.

Myers It's my fault for snooping.

Anne We're not usually like this, I swear.

Myers When you've got a front door you'll have a bit more privacy. Where
should I start?

Anne Start with a cup of tea. I'll make it. (*She turns toward the kitchen*)

Guy enters from the kitchen

Myers Hi, Guy.

Guy Hi, Myers. What are you doing here? Did I leave something at the
office?

Myers No. It's Sunday. I said I'd help you paint the house.

Guy Where's all the air in here? Can we open a window? There's no air in
here!

Anne There's air, honey, the window's open.

Guy Do you smell something?

Anne No.

Guy There's a smell in here that won't go away. (*To Myers*) Do you smell
it?

Myers No.

Guy I hate the shape of this room.

Anne I love it.

Guy You saw the drawings, why didn't you tell me it was going to feel this
way? So tight, so ——

Anne Relax, Guy.

Myers I'll go make the tea. I want to! You two kiss and make up or whatever it is nearly-weds do. Me, I can't remember.

Myers exits through to the kitchen

Guy I'm sorry, Anne, I haven't been sleeping.

Anne I know her death has been hard on you. I've understood that. But there's something else, isn't there? You look at me out the corner of your eye. You never did that before. Without turning your head. It sends a chill through me.

Guy Let's forget it, all right?

Anne No. Sometimes, if we're both reading, I look up at you and smile, and you nearly jump like I've caught you doing something you shouldn't be doing. You treat me like I'm an intruder. It never used to be like that. What did I say in there?

Guy Nothing, Anne, it's me ...

Anne It obviously upset you ——

Guy You just keep going on about the Palmyra, the Palmyra, I'm sick of hearing the word!

Anne I'm proud of you!

Guy Well don't be.

Anne All I said was if you never built another thing, your spirit would live forever in the Palmyra.

Guy *I don't want it to live in the Palmyra!* The Palmyra's over, it's finished, can I move onto something else now or is the Palmyra going to be the stone at the head of my grave? I'll tell you, Anne, if I thought the Palmyra was the last thing I'd ever build, I'd take a train there right now and jump off the top of it.

Anne Don't say that.

Guy And anyway, I'm going to do an office building for Shaw Realty. They've seen my work and they say it's going ahead.

Anne An office building!

Guy They're drawing up the contracts now.

Anne Where's it going to be?

Guy Manhattan.

Anne Manhattan! Guy, why didn't you tell me?

Guy It was going to be a surprise, a present for our wedding, but if it'll keep the word Palmyra out of this house ——

Anne Oh honey, I promise! I'll never say the word again. Where are the drawings?

Guy They're at the office.

Anne I want to see them!

Guy There's nothing to see. It's just a building.

Anne Just a building! I never thought I'd hear you talk like that!

Guy Like what? It's a building. A job.

Anne Come here.

Guy I don't ——

Anne Shhhh. Baby, is there something wrong? Something you're not telling me?

Guy No...

Anne Would you tell me if there was?

Guy Of course.

Anne Are you sure?

He takes her hand

Guy You're my glass of reality. Sometimes I look at things with your eyes and it helps me see them the right way. But it's not working just now so you'll have to be patient with me. I need to get down to some work. There's nothing else that'll help me now. Not even you.

Myers puts his head around the corner

Myers Phone for you, Guy.

Guy Who is it?

Myers He wouldn't say. He said it was a surprise.

Guy Tell him I'm not here. I don't want any surprises.

The Lights cross-fade to the next scene

SCENE 6

The stairs at R

Bruno appears at the bottom of the stairs, teetering drunkenly, holding a pencil and paper. He mounts the stairs, counting the steps on the way up

Bruno One, two, three, four, five, six, seven, eight, nine, ten, eleven, twelve, thirteen, fourteen, fifteen, sixteen. Sixteen. (*He writes this down, and begins a slow descent*) Dear Guy. The first thing you do is take out the gun. It's beautiful, elegant and compact, a minor masterpiece of architecture! You put the bullets in the chamber and stick the gun in your pocket, and in your other pocket you put the key to our back door. I sent it to you in a previous letter! I trust you received it? The lock on the back door is broken, but take the key with you in case they've had it mended by then. Take the train to Great Neck Station. Go out the first exit and on to the main road, walk a hundred and twenty-seven paces to the footpath, and turn right.

Sixty paces along the path is a lamp with an oily gold and blue halo. It marks a gate. Open the gate. Twenty-two paces up from the gate is a wall. Jump over the wall. And there, in the dark, you'll see the house.

He is halfway down the stairs now. He reels and nearly falls, but he regains balance. He looks up the stairs

Sixteen steps up to your room, Daddy, how do you like that? I wish you were home now so you could see what I was doing, because guess what, *Guy Haines is going to kill you! and guess who's helping him?* (*With disgust*) You don't know who I am. (*During the following, he comes slowly downstairs. He faces front again. As though to reporters*) Yes, these are the hands that did it, I squeezed the life right out of her just because I decided to do it, but there's something else nobody knows about: when I was at her I thought, now I've been where Guy has been, not in the same way, but I was there too, just like he was, just like Guy. And you know what? We may go other places too, once the captain's gone and I get my *own goddamn money*, we're going to go to other places together, just me and Guy, we're going to get a boat and sail around the world teaching people how to *live*! Yeah, these are the hands that did it, but I owe it to him, because when I got off that train in Metcalf I thought this is the state where Guy was born, and because I was there too I thought I could do anything in the world, and my spirit working for him would be immortal, like his, and like him I'd live forever, next to him I'd live forever.

He sobs drunkenly, briefly, but soon regains composure. He is now at the bottom of the stairs

The butler's room is on the first landing, by the grandfather clock. This is the closest you'll come to anyone. You'll hear the ticking of the clock. The landing squeaks in the middle, so remember to wait for the clock to strike the hour. That's when you run across the landing, while the clock's chiming, to hide the squeak in the floor. My father's door will be just on your right.

The Lights come up dimly in Guy's room, a tiny apartment space with a kitchenette concealed behind a curtain. The curtain is drawn shut

Guy is sitting on his bed, reading a letter

You follow the snoring. If there is a moon, you will see the shape of his head against the pillow. You take the gun from your pocket and aim it at his head. It is not a person. It is a target. And remember: You've done this many times before. This is only one of the times.

Bruno exits

The Lights go down on the stair area

Guy crumples the letter and throws it into the wastebasket. He changes his mind, goes back to the wastebasket, take the letter out and smooths it, refolds it, puts it back in its envelope, and puts the envelope in the bottom drawer of his dresser. He goes to the mirror above his bureau and looks at himself

He grabs his coat and leaves the room, turning the lights out after him

SCENE 7

Guy's office

As the Lights come up a large envelope slides in under the door. There is stillness for some time

Then, in the street by a public telephone, Bruno appears. He dials the phone. The phone in Guy's office begins to ring

It rings several times before Guy appears at the door in his coat. He moves toward the phone just as Myers appears through the other entrance, coming in to answer the phone as well

Guy I'll get it. (*He answers the phone*) Guy Haines.
Bruno I want to talk to you, Guy.
Guy (*nervous*) No, I'm sorry. It's not. (*He hangs up*)
Myers The phone's been going non-stop. I think there's something wrong with the line. Half the time I answer it there's no-one there.
Guy Has Shaw Realty called?
Myers No.
Guy God *damn it*, when are they going to call? (*He removes his coat*)
Myers The contracts have already gone to their legal department.
Guy How do you know?
Myers I play tennis with Doug Frear. Trust me. It's going ahead.

Guy sits at his desk and puts his head in his hands. During the following, Bruno dials again

Why don't you go home and get some sleep? You look like you haven't been to bed in weeks.

Guy I don't want sleep, I want work!

Myers The lunchtime drinks aren't going to help.

Guy I'm not drinking at lunchtime!

Myers I'm not judging you, I've done it myself. I'm saying it doesn't work.

Guy I had three martinis yesterday at lunch, what difference does it make to you? You rent space off me, I don't need advice about the way I run my life.

Guy's phone rings. Myers picks it up

Myers Frank Myers, hallo.

Silence. Bruno hangs up

I could hear the street this time. Somebody's there but he's not talking.

Myers puts the phone down. The light on Bruno goes out

Bruno exits

Guy I'm sorry, Myers. Not knowing is driving me crazy. I feel like I've been circling and circling in the air, waiting to land.

Myers Just get some sleep. I promise to track you down if they call.

Bruno appears DL, looking upward as though at an office window

Guy Do you hear something?

Myers Like what?

Guy Shhh!

Pause. They listen. Guy relaxes, and so does Myers

The light in here is too bright.

Myers (*moving toward his own table, muttering*) Or too dim. Or smells weird. Or makes a funny noise. (*En route, he kicks the envelope on the floor. He picks it up and reads it*) Hey, look at this! "To the greatest architect in the world!" (*He laughs*) Question is, which one of us is it for? (*He opens it and unfolds a large drawing*) It's a drawing. "A house in Great Neck." Look, it's got all the measurements of the property, but in paces, not in feet! Ha ha! Twenty-two paces from the gate to the back wall, thirty-five paces from the wall to the side of the house, nineteen paces along the side of the house to the back door ...

Myers laughs. Guy tries to take the drawing from him

Guy (*pretending to laugh with him*) Here, let me see that ...

Myers pulls it away from him

Myers Eleven paces from the kitchen door to the side stairs. "Do not use main stairs — they all squeak"! Ha ha ha!

Guy It's from my friend Robert Treacher, I'm sure of it. He used to play jokes like this all the time back in college. Let me have it!

Myers Hang on! "See note" ... Where's note? "Don't forget when you climb the stairs that the fourth and seventh stairs squeak, and also the top of the landing, so remember to 'skip four, skip seven, and step wide at the top' — you can remember that, it's got a syncopated rhythm". Ha ha ha! Skip four, skip seven, step wide at the top! Skip four, skip seven, step wide at the top!

Guy finally manages to grab the drawing. Myer's mirth subsides

Guy Yeah, that's Treacher's handwriting, I'm sure of it. He lives up in Canada now. (*He puts it back in the envelope, puts the envelope in his coat pocket, puts on his coat, and moves toward the door*)

Myers Well, he's in town at the moment. There's no stamp on it.

Guy goes out the door

The Lights go down on the office

Guy appears DR, looking for Bruno. He sees him at the other side of the stage, and rushes at him

Guy Why don't you just die and *leave me alone*?!

Bruno (*defending himself*) Don't hurt me, Guy ——

Guy I knew you'd be down here!

Bruno I want to know what you do, where you are!

Guy I can't go down the street without seeing you out the corner of my eye! The phone's always ringing, you're driving me *insane*!

Bruno When are you going to do it, Guy?

Guy *I'm not going to do it!*

Bruno We made a deal!

Guy *You* made a deal, you do it yourself!

Bruno It'll be so easy, I've done all the planning ...

Guy I know! I've been getting your insane letters ...

Bruno I never miss a day, do I, Guy?

Guy I don't want them any more, I've had *enough* ...

Bruno You need them so when you finally do what they say it'll be so familiar it won't be like something new you're doing, it'll be like something you've done a hundred times before!

Guy *I don't need any more letters!* I already know what's in them, I know them better than I know my own thoughts! I know which train to take to Great Neck; how to jump over the wall and run diagonally across the back lawn to avoid the cracking twigs; what to do when I get to the back door: if it's open, if it's closed, if it's locked; I know the cold of the kitchen tiles; I know the shapes of everything and where it all is in the dark, the tables and the chairs; I know the steps that squeak and the sound of the ticking and the chiming of the clock; the sound of the snoring; the head on the pillow; the breeze through the window — *I've had enough!*

Bruno You *have* had enough. You've had enough time.

Guy No more, no more ...

Bruno You can finish it.

Guy Every shred of me is proof against this thing!

Bruno Yes, and you're wasting away, Guy. I'll have to crack down for your own good.

Guy The answer is no ...

Bruno You have till Friday. If you don't say yes by Friday, I'm writing to Anne.

Guy To Anne?

Bruno You didn't think I'd find out about her, did you?

Guy Please leave her out of this!

Bruno Why didn't you tell me about her?

Guy Tell you?

Bruno On the train. Why didn't you tell me about her on the train?

Guy What do you know about her?

Bruno Well I know everything now. What don't I know about Anne Faulkner?

A gentle light comes up in Guy's room

Anne enters the room

I probably know things you don't know yourself. And I know one thing for sure. She's not the sort of woman who'd marry a murderer.

Guy I'm not a murderer...

Bruno You've got till Friday to say yes, or I'm writing to Anne.

Guy She's got nothing to do with you!

Bruno She does, Guy. I think she does.

Bruno walks off down the street, and Guy goes in the other direction

The Lights go down on the street area

SCENE 8

Guy's room

The Lights come up more fully on Guy's room. The curtain to the kitchenette is half-drawn

Anne is now on the bed looking through Guy's old sketchbooks

Guy opens the front door with his keys and is shocked at first when he sees her

Anne I didn't mean to startle you.

Guy How did you get in?

Anne The key behind the drainpipe. Don't worry, I put it back.

Guy I thought you hated it here.

Anne I wanted to see you.

Guy Has the phone been ringing?

Anne No. Are you expecting a call?

Guy No.

Anne Let me make you a cup of tea. (*She stands*)

Guy I'm not good company tonight.

Anne Quick cup of tea, then I'll go. (*She draws back the curtain of the kitchenette and begins to make tea*)

Guy (*indicating the books on the bed*) What were you doing here?

Anne Just going through your old sketchbooks.

Guy Why?

Anne I wanted to know what you were like before I met you. The drawings are good.

Guy Better than I could do now.

Anne Now you only draw what you're going to build. In those books you drew any old thing — the Staten Island Ferry, workmen digging the road, you even drew Radio City Music Hall twice, once as it was, and once with improvements!

Guy (*putting the books back on the shelf*) I was a student.

Anne I even found one of your old essays. (*She lifts a notebook; reading*) "A house should reflect the habits of the people who live in it. For instance, will the child wish to pause at the window before he climbs the sixteen steps to his bedroom to sleep?"

A dim light comes up on the stairs at R

Guy is staring at himself in the mirror. He jerks himself back to reality and the light on the stairs goes out

Guy I want to work now. I want to work now.
Anne Why don't you turn your attention to something else?
Guy Like what?
Anne There's the house. Why don't you go stay at the house?
Guy It's not possible.
Anne Why not? Look at this place! It's your old life. Go work on the house, and stay there.
Guy I can't work on the house. Something's in the way.
Anne What's in the way?
Guy The Palmyra's all I'm ever going to build. That's the joke. But who's laughing, huh? Who's laughing?
Anne What's happening, Guy?
Guy What do you mean?
Anne Something's going on, something you're not talking about. Tell me, Guy.
Guy Nothing's going on.
Anne I got a letter today.
Guy (*freezing*) From who?
Anne I don't know. It's about you. I'll read it to you. (*She takes it out of her pocket and reads*) "Dear Miss Faulkner: No doubt it will interest you to know that your fiancé, Mr Guy Daniel Haines, played a greater role in the death of his wife than the world at present thinks. In any event, he will not remain a free man much longer, because the truth will soon be revealed. This is not a joke. This is from one who knows."

Guy takes the letter

Guy Do you have the envelope?

She takes the envelope from her pocket and he snatches it

Anne Grand Central Station. Who sent it, Guy?
Guy How would I know?
Anne I have the feeling you do.
Guy There was probably some lunatic at the inquest.
Anne You're not protecting me?
Guy From what?
Anne That's what I'm asking!

Guy You don't believe that letter, do you?

Anne Of course not!

Guy You couldn't believe that letter and still be planning to marry me, could you? What kind of a monster would I have to be to have a death on my soul and to be walking around, smiling, telling you I love you, when I'd be cut off from that forever? That's what they mean by hell, Anne. Not somewhere else. That.

The phone begins to ring. Neither moves. Eventually Anne goes toward it

It's my phone!

Anne is shocked. She goes to the kitchen and turns off the cooker, drawing the curtain shut. She gathers her things

Anne It's a choice to be alone, Guy. Just remember that.

She goes out the door, closing it behind her

Guy bursts into tears of anger. He turns off the lights and paces around in the dark with his hands to his ears, blocking out the phone which continues to ring and ring. Finally he grabs the receiver out of its cradle

Guy (*shouting into the phone*) Die, just *die*, will you? *Die!* (*He sobs, listening*) I can't ... You know I can't, Bruno ... Don't make me do it ... The answer is no. (*He hangs up*)

He gets his coat and goes out

The Lights cross-fade to the next scene

SCENE 9

Bruno's bedroom

Bruno searches for a bottle, finds one, drinks from it, wipes his mouth with his sleeve, puts the cap on the bottle and slips it in his overnight bag, which is nearly full, on his bed. He takes the Plato book out from under the mattress, sits on the bed for a moment reading it. After a time he closes the book and puts it in his bag

Elsie appears in the doorway

Elsie How long will you be gone?

Bruno Just a few days.

Elsie Do you know where you're going?

Bruno Palm Beach, Florida. I'm going to join a country club.

Elsie That's a long way to go for a country club. It must be a special one.

Bruno You've never seen anything like it, Ma. It's beautiful, the way temples were beautiful in the days when people still believed in things.

Elsie I wish I could come.

Bruno Come.

Elsie It's the spring party this weekend, the only time all year your father asks me to be here.

Bruno Get out of it. For me. We'll knock 'em dead in Florida — they'll think you're my girlfriend, not my mother! They always do!

Elsie I don't think we can pull that one off any more.

Bruno Of course we can!

Elsie Baby, I'm too old.

Elsie looks at the photographs on the wall

Where has all the time gone? Look at you in your little sailor suit! You used to love dressing up for me.

Bruno Remember when you taught me the foxtrot?

Elsie (*laughing*) You were only this high, but you loved to dance with your mother.

Bruno I still do!

Bruno holds out his hand to her

Come sit by me, Ma.

She takes his hand and sits. He reclines with his head in her lap. She strokes his hair

Elsie You had such rosy cheeks. All the women used to say, a boy with such rosy cheeks — it's a crime! Remember when you brought me a bouquet of flowers from the garden?

Bruno I was only five, wasn't I Ma?

Elsie You pulled them out by the roots.

Bruno Dad hit me because of it.

Elsie He gave you a little spanking. He was just trying to teach you.

Bruno He taught me.

They are both silent for a time

Elsie I used to hold my baby like this and sing to him — do you remember?
Bruno Are you kidding? That's the only thing worth remembering.
Elsie You remember what I sang?
Bruno Sing now, Ma.
Elsie (*singing*)   Beautiful dreamer, wake unto me,
                    Starlight and dewdrops are waiting for thee,
                    Sounds of the rude world heard in the day,
                    Lull'd by the moonlight have all passed away...
    (*She stops singing and searches his face*) You've changed.

Bruno stands and goes over to his bag. He clasps it up and hefts it on to his shoulder

    You've met someone, haven't you?

He watches her, then goes to her and kisses her on the forehead

Bruno Bye, Mom. (*He goes toward the door*)
Elsie (*calling after him*) Don't leave me alone here for long.

    Bruno exits with his bag

The Lights cross-fade to the next scene

SCENE 10

The Haines's living-room

Anne comes in through the front door carrying overnight bags. She looks around, puts down her things. She goes to the phone and dials

The Lights come up dimly in Guy's room. He is lying on his bed in the dark, fully dressed. The telephone is off the hook. He is humming gently to himself, as if total silence might invite the sound of a phone ringing. The curtain is closed across the kitchenette

Anne hangs up and sits on the couch near the phone. The Lights fade on her

Myers appears at Guy's door and knocks

Myers Guy?

Guy jumps like a frightened animal, looks at the door, searches desperately around him and hides behind the bed, staring at the door

Guy, are you in there? There's something wrong with your phone. I couldn't get through. I've heard from Shaw Realty, Guy. About the job.

Guy considers, stands, looks at himself in the mirror, combs his hair with his fingers, moves to the door and opens it hesitantly

The news isn't good. They've gone with another architect. I'm sorry. I thought the contract was just a formality, but ... Well, what happened was, they received a letter. It was about you. It said you were partly to blame for ... what happened to your wife. They're sure it was just a crank, but they know what the press would do with something like that, and they're pumping a lot of money into this project. They don't want to take the risk.

Guy says nothing

You couldn't do the job anyway, could you. Look at you.

Myers turns to go

You're a good man, Guy. Get yourself looked after.

Myers goes

Guy shuts the door behind him and moves to the bureau where he lights a candle which is in front of the mirror. He takes the metal wastebasket over to the bureau, takes a few letters from the drawer, and burns them one by one at the candle, throwing them into the wastebasket. He goes back to the drawer and takes out a few more letters, tears them and throws them into the wastebasket. He goes back to the drawer and takes out an enormous stack of letters in their envelopes, a hundred at least, and haphazardly tears them, sobbing, dropping to his knees, putting some in the wastebasket, a snow of torn envelopes littering the floor around him

He crawls back to the bedside table, opens the top drawer, and takes out the gun. He holds the gun up, checks to see that it is loaded, and closes the chamber, staring at it in wonder. He brings the gun to his face, feels its coldness, sobs

The curtain of the kitchenette is drawn back and Bruno is there

Bruno It'll all be over soon.

Guy I know.
Bruno Now it's going to be easy.
Guy I know.

Bruno gets down on his knees with Guy and looks him in the eyes

Bruno You're ready now, aren't you, Guy?
Guy (*fresh sobbing; relief*) Yes …
Bruno You'll never see me again.
Guy I will.
Bruno No. This is the last time.

Guy grabs Bruno and embraces him tightly, sobbing

Guy Please!
Bruno I'll be gone, but I'll be with you in your head. Just remember, you've
done this many times before.
Guy This is only one of the times.
Bruno You see? Everybody's got that thing inside them, the thing that can
do it …
Guy Mine is you.
Bruno Yours is you.

Bruno stands and goes out the door

Guy moves to the mirror and stares at his face in the candlelight

*A gentle light comes up in Bruno's bedroom, where Elsie stands, looking
at a family photograph on the wall*

*The Lights come up in the Haines's living-room, where Anne sits on the couch
near the phone*

Bruno appears DR, *and he begins to walk slowly across the stage, dreamily,
counting his paces. He reaches downstage of his own bedroom*

*Elsie turns away from the photograph and leaves the room, switching the
lights off as she leaves*

Bruno reaches downstage of Guy's room

*Guy puts on his coat, puts the gun in his pocket, blows out the candle, and
goes out*

Bruno reaches downstage of Anne

Anne dials Guy once more, listens, puts the phone down, gathers her things and leaves the house, turning off the lights as she goes out

Bruno is now at the other side of the stage and he exits

The stage is in darkness now. A dim light rises on the stairs at R

Guy enters R, *slowly, quietly, defeated. He stops at the bottom of the stairs and takes out the gun. Quietly, he weeps, careful not to make a sound. He recovers and looks up the stairs. He begins to climb them slowly. He skips the fourth step. He skips the seventh step. At the landing, he waits for the clock to chime. When it does, he steps wide at the top and disappears into the darkness*

CURTAIN

ACT II

SCENE 1

The Haines's living-room

The Lights come up on the Haines's living room, which is now finished and furnished. Music drifts in from off stage: a wedding reception in the garden

Anne leads Guy by the hand into the living-room. They have just been married, and Anne is in white

Anne (*calling*) Is there anyone in here?

She looks around. No response

Good.
Guy What are we doing?
Anne I just want to be alone with you for a moment.
Guy They'll wonder where we've gone.
Anne Let them wonder. Kiss me. Wait! Little kisses. Forehead.

He kisses her forehead

Elbow.

He kisses her elbow

Nose.

He kisses her nose

Finger.

He kisses her finger

Lips.

They kiss

What's this?

Guy What?

Anne You've got a scar on your neck.

Guy It's just a scratch.

Anne And there's a bruise under your ear!

Guy (*covering his face with his hands*) Anne ——

Anne And here's a cut on your hand! What happened to you, Guy?

Guy Nothing happened.

Anne How did you get these cuts and bruises?

Guy I was playing football.

Anne You never play football!

Guy I do!

Anne Don't lie to me. We're married now, it's a mortal sin to lie to me! You've been fighting, haven't you?

Guy I haven't been fighting. I never fight.

Robert Treacher enters

Treacher Oh there you are.

Anne Robert, have you ever known Guy to play football?

Treacher Football! Guy?!

Guy Thanks for the vote of confidence.

Treacher (*to Anne*) Your father's looking for you.

Anne Oh. I promised him a dance with the bride. (*To Guy*) And no fights while I'm gone!

Anne goes

Treacher The thought of you having a fight!

Guy Isn't she beautiful?

Treacher Listen Guy, I've got to tell you something. I know it might not be the right moment, but I've got to fly back tonight and I wanted to talk to you before I go.

Guy Have you got a drink?

Treacher Listen! I've been appointed to the Alberta Bridge Project up in Edmonton. It's the most beautiful place in the world, and they're building a bridge over the North Saskatchewan River. They even want it to be white.

Guy Yeah?

Treacher It's a bridge, Guy, just what you've always wanted to build. They even want it to be white!

Guy How do you know they'd have me?

Treacher I've already put your name forward. Acceptance is guaranteed.

Guy I'd have to spend a lot of time up there.

Treacher For the first six months.

Guy I just got married.

Treacher So? Anne's not the type to mind you doing what you've dreamt about all your life, is she?

Guy I don't know if it's my dream anymore.

Treacher It was always your dream!

Guy Well I've changed.

Treacher *I don't believe it.*

Guy Honest, I have.

Treacher But you never let up about it at college! You were going to build a white bridge, with a ——

Guy ⎫
Treacher ⎭ (*together*) — span like an angel's wing ...

Treacher It was what you dreamed about ever since you were a kid! I was your roommate! I had to listen to you go on about it night after night, I had to live with a half a dozen models at any one time all over the living-room and the table where we were supposed to eat, it's what made you become an architect in the first place, Guy, seeing the bridge at Schiers — what's changed?

Guy I don't think it's me any more.

Treacher It was all you were about! If it's not you any more, what is there left of you?

Guy I don't know.

Treacher What happened?

Guy Maybe I've just grown up.

Treacher I don't believe that. Come on, Guy, it wasn't just an adolescent fancy, it was the thing that drove you through all those years at college, everybody knew about you and your white bridge! As soon as the rumours began up north, it had your name written all over it, and you're not going to let me down, because I haven't let you down, Guy, I thought of you, I remembered! And if you're going to say no after all I've done to set this up, you can at least promise to give it some thought. Will you do that, Guy? Will you think about it?

Myers enters with Anne. He has a camera with a flashlight

Myers All right, you and you, by the fireplace with the bride.

Anne Picture time! Bride in the middle.

Myers Husband on your left ...

Anne Smiling, honey.

Treacher, Guy and Anne position themselves to be photographed by Myers. Myers is focusing the camera

Bruno, with a drink in his hand, appears behind him

Guy loses his smile

   I said smiling!

Guy fakes it as best he can

Myers All right, nearly ready ...

Flash. They applaud and disperse

Anne Frank Myers, have you met Robert Treacher, our best man?
Myers No, we haven't met ... but I know his work!
Treacher You do?
Myers (*laughing*) The work you do on houses! Skip four, skip seven ...
Treacher What?
Myers Step wide at the top! Ha ha! I like your sense of humour! I hope you
   don't get nervous making public speeches.
Treacher (*confused*) No no, I'll... be too drunk to be nervous.
Myers That's what we like to hear.
Treacher I'll go practise, just to take the edge off it. (*To Guy*) I'll be on the
   porch if you need me!

   Treacher disappears

*Myers starts to change the film in his camera. Bruno approaches Guy, mildly
drunk*

Bruno Hallo, Guy. I've come to offer you my best wishes.

Silence

Anne Ignore Mr Etiquette here. I'm Anne Haines.
Bruno Aren't you going to introduce me to your wife, Guy?
Guy Anne, this is Charles Bruno.
Anne Pleased to meet you.
Bruno Mrs Haines, I think you're the most beautiful bride I've ever seen.
Anne And you must have seen thousands!
Bruno I have!
Anne How do you know Guy?
Bruno Oh, I've known Guy just about all his life. Haven't I, Guy?
Guy That's right, yes.

Bruno You could even say I'm the closest friend he's ever had. Isn't that true, Guy?

Guy Yes, it is.

Anne He's never mentioned you before. Where did you meet?

Bruno Where was it, Guy?

Guy At the Parker Art Institute?

Bruno I think it may have been there.

Anne Did you study there?

Bruno Me? No, I ——

Guy Mr Bruno doesn't work.

Bruno I do work!

Anne Well which is it? Do you work, or don't you?

Bruno I work. It's just not the sort of work you can see with the naked eye.

Anne He's a thinker.

Bruno That's what I am! A thinker!

Anne And what are you thinking right now?

Bruno I'm thinking how lucky we are to have found each other in such a big, big world!

Myers has succeeded in changing the film

Myers All right, the gentlemen alone, and then I'll set up for the speeches. (*To Anne*) Will you help me read the light?

Anne I will. Will you take one of me by the pond, all alone?

Myers (*as a bridegroom*) I do.

Anne (*clapping to move them*) All right, the men by themselves, come on, last one in the house, then we go outside!

Bruno enthusiastically moves into position to have his picture taken with Guy, but Guy hesitates

Move it, boys!

Guy moves next to Bruno

Myers Arms around each other.

Bruno puts his arm merrily around Guy

And ...

Flash. Anne applauds. Myers moves to go

Anne (*to Guy*) Don't you disappear now. They can't make the speeches without you!

Anne follows Myers out

Bruno and Guy are left alone

Guy I thought I was never going to see you again.
Bruno Aw, Guy ——
Guy Get *out*!
Bruno It's a time for celebration!
Guy I thought I was free of you!
Bruno I had to applaud you. You were perfect, you did it without a hitch!
Guy Not without a hitch! I ran the wrong way in the woods and got caught up in the trees! I've got scars and bruises! Anne's noticed!
Bruno But it's just as I said, Guy — the police don't know where to begin! You did leave something behind, but the gods being on our side, I found it before they did. (*He takes the revolver out of his pocket*)
Guy Put that away!
Bruno I found it in the woods.
Guy Get rid of it!

Bruno puts it back in his pocket

Bruno It was like a message from you. I saw it shining and it was like light in the grass. Like you were talking to me in a way only I could understand. A promise kept, shining in the grass. I felt so close to you. I feel so close to you. I couldn't stay away!
Guy You've ruined the plan!
Bruno I haven't ruined it, Guy.
Guy Two strangers on a train who've never even met — it was going to drive the cops in all different directions!
Bruno It has!
Guy But you've come to my house!
Bruno They haven't followed me.
Guy What about all the people here? Now we've been seen together by all the people here, there's even a picture of us together!
Bruno It won't be in the papers, Guy — stop worrying! People aren't as clever as you think.
Guy The police haven't given up yet.
Bruno They haven't got the minds to find us! Things get thrown together by accident, then they come apart again. You can't untangle the world, it's too much of a mess, unless you use logic, and the world's not held together by

logic, so nobody can sniff their way to us. Besides, our deeds are charmed, Guy. We're immortal. You'll just have to accept the fact that we got away with it.

Guy I got away with nothing. All the spirit has left me. I'm alone.

Bruno Neither of us is ever alone anymore.

Guy I am. I am.

Bruno Things are better than they were before — and I have my money, it's *our* money, Guy!

Guy I don't want money! Not from you.

Bruno Guy...

Guy I had one person against me, one! Now I have them all, all men and all women, all of them past, present and future, in their eyes I will see myself and *I will always be this thing*! My hell has got as small as my skin. That's what I got from you.

Anne enters

Anne They're about to do the toast.

Bruno I'll go fill up my glass.

Guy I thought you weren't going to stay for the speeches.

Bruno I wouldn't miss them for the world! They're about you, my hero and my friend! Let me salute you, Guy, and you, Anne Haines... may we all live a long and peaceful and contented life together. (*He holds up his glass*) To that. *To that!*

Bruno clinks his glass against the wall and winks at Guy, then disappears

Anne He's a bit drunk, your friend.

Guy I know.

Anne Has he upset you?

Guy No!

Anne Have I?

Guy No...

Anne Are you sorry you married me?

Guy No.

Anne Then kiss me, big kiss — and promise to let me make you happy.

They kiss, then Anne leads him out

The Lights cross-fade to the next scene

SCENE 2

Gerard's office

Gerard sits behind his desk, and Bruno stands before it

Bruno What are you still doing here? Haven't you heard? Your employer's dead.

Gerard Your mother's asked me to stay on.

Bruno Well I'm not answering any of your questions.

Gerard Charley ——

Bruno I never said you could call me Charley!

Gerard I was hoping you could help.

Bruno Help what? Why are you here? Why is she keeping you on?

Gerard Because some people are concerned about your father's death.

Bruno I'm concerned about my father's death! But if we need a private investigator I'd vote for getting a good one!

Gerard I knew him best, his habits, his friends ...

Bruno Well I'm going to talk to my mother about this. I don't see why we should keep my dad's minder on the payroll when he's not even alive to mind!

Gerard It's not the money, Charles. I'd work on this case for nothing. Your father was my friend.

Bruno You were his staff. He didn't have any friends he didn't pay for.

Gerard You didn't know your father.

Bruno I know he hated me.

Gerard That's where you're wrong.

Bruno Well maybe you don't know everything either. Have you ever thought of that?

Gerard I thought you'd be more co-operative.

Bruno I'd like to go see my mother. In case you haven't noticed, she's not well.

Gerard I have noticed, and I hope she gets better soon. There are some questions I'd like to ask her.

Bruno Are you made of dead wood or something? *She's not well!*

Gerard Charles, I think the murderer may have known the layout of this house.

Bruno Oh, that narrows it down! We've only given eight hundred parties!

Gerard I'm saying I think he had a bit of help.

Bruno From who?

Gerard I didn't say I knew that.

Bruno Then what are you implying?

Gerard I'm implying nothing. I'm just wondering why things were so easy for him.

Bruno Like what?

Gerard There was a milk crate under the wall.

Bruno So? The milk crate's by the cherry tree. I've got a birdhouse in the cherry tree. I need to stand on the milk crate to check if there's any birds in there. What's wrong with that?

Gerard Nothing. You just never showed any interest in birds until two days before the murder.

Bruno You think I helped the murderer?

Gerard I'm just asking, Charles. Also the lock on the back door was broken.

Bruno Some clue! It was like that for two months!

Gerard Was it?

Bruno Didn't you know that? Well you should've known that and fixed it yourself! Then maybe you'd have been worth the money he paid you!

Gerard You don't seem to understand, Charles, I'm on your side.

Bruno A lot *that's* worth! A failed cop on my very own side, what on earth did I do to deserve it? This is a waste of time.

Bruno heads for the door

Gerard What's your connection with Mrs Guy Haines?

Bruno (*freezing*) Why do you ask that?

Gerard I notice from your cash accounts you've sent her some flowers.

Bruno So? I was sick at her wedding. I sent her some flowers to apologize.

Gerard How do you know her?

Bruno I'm a friend of her husband's.

Gerard Have you known him long?

Bruno He was one of the architects we thought of when we were talking about building a house.

Gerard When were you talking about building a house?

Bruno Last year.

Gerard Who's we?

Bruno Me and my mother.

Gerard Without your father?

Bruno My father too.

Gerard He never mentioned it to me.

Bruno All right, my mother and I talked about it in private, we were going to build it as a surprise for Dad, all right? We were just discussing it, like we discuss a lot of things. We discuss taking trips, too, and we don't tell Dad about them. Why should we? Most trips we don't even take, just like the house we never built! Is it a crime to talk? (*He moves toward the door*) I'm going to see that my mother releases you from this assignment.

Gerard I'm going to ask her about that house.
Bruno *She's not well!* Have you no decency? Why don't you just go back
to the donut shop you crawled out of? Civilians have manners. *You don't
belong!*

Bruno exits, slamming the door behind him

The Lights cross-fade to the next scene

SCENE 3

The Haines's living-room

Anne comes in from the kitchen with a vase of exotic flowers

Anne But this is exactly where they ought to be, out here where we can see
them. It's not often we have such beautiful flowers in the house!

Guy follows her in, wearing his suit from work

Guy I don't want to look at them.
Anne Why not?
Guy I don't like them.
Anne It's not that you don't like the flowers. You don't like the person who
sent them.
Guy Charles Bruno is a lonely drunk, he's not even worth the effort to dislike.
Anne Then be gracious and accept his gift!
Guy Anne ...

Anne sets them down and fusses with them

Anne There. See? They're beautiful. Why don't you go change? I don't like
the look of you in a suit.
Guy Well you better get used to it. Knapp and Hanson have offered me a job.
Anne So? You get offered jobs all the time. (*She stops arranging the flowers
and turns to him*) Guy? You're not going to take it!
Guy I'm thinking about it.
Anne You can't be!
Guy Why not? It would be nice to be on the clock for a while.
Anne But you said you'd never take a job with a firm!
Guy Maybe I've changed my mind. I've enjoyed supervising the drawings
for the hospital. They appreciate me there, and I don't have to think. The
day's over before I know it.

Anne Why should you want the day to be over?

Guy It's work, Anne. Everybody wants it to be over.

Anne It wasn't just work to you before.

Guy It's work to me now.

Anne I don't believe you.

Guy Believe me. I'd like the security of a firm.

Anne You built the Palmyra, Guy!

Guy I know.

Anne You don't have the temperament for a firm! They'll have you doing drawings!

Guy I like to draw. You know when you get it right and when you get it wrong. You sit down and do the job, and if it measures up, it's done. You clock out, go home, and you're not an architect any more, at least not till nine o'clock the next morning. That may not sound appealing to you, but it sounds appealing to me.

Anne What are you trying to hide from, Guy?

Guy Nothing.

Anne With you the work was never finished. Not when we first met. You were always sketching, even sometimes when we were out for dinner you'd sketch something on a napkin, you never stopped wanting to make things, to build things. You dreamt of things to build all day and all night long. You had the touch. You'd reach out and put some things together, things that weren't beautiful on their own, things that didn't go together, and you would put them together and make them beautiful, you'd make beauty — not everyone can do it, Guy. If you have it, you've got to use it.

Guy I don't have it any more.

Anne Is it Treacher's job you're afraid of?

Guy Have you been speaking to him?

Anne He called three times today.

Guy So he's told you about the bridge.

Anne Aren't you going to do it, Guy?

Guy Do you want me to be going back and forth to Canada for six months?

Anne Yes I do, of course I do!

Guy I can't build a bridge.

Anne Guy, look at me.

Guy *You look at me!* Look at my eyes. Do you see anything in there that could build a bridge?

She stares in his eyes, silently

You think I'm the man I was when you met me, well look again. If there was a bridge in there, it's not there any more. It's gone. Dead. The game's over. I can't pretend any more. I'm no longer inspired. I'm taking a job with a firm. And I don't like flowers.

He throws the flowers into the fireplace and starts to take off his tie as he goes off

The Lights cross-fade to the next scene

SCENE 4

Gerard's office

Elsie is sitting across from Gerard. She is smoking, distracted

Gerard He didn't seem in particularly high or low spirits?
Elsie He's a very moody boy. I doubt if I'd have noticed.
Gerard Do you think there's anything he's not telling me?
Elsie Do you?
Gerard He was acting strangely about that time.
Elsie He was acting strangely about every time. He's a strange boy. But Charles wants you to find the murderer as much as I do. He loved his father.
Gerard I expected him to be more co-operative.
Elsie He dislikes authority.
Gerard Has he told you anything?
Elsie What would he tell me? You think he knows something about this?
Gerard I'm asking you.
Elsie Arthur, my boy doesn't know anything about this. He's lost his father. He's grieving and he's confused. If he's said anything ——
Gerard He hasn't said anything.
Elsie And he won't. He won't.
Gerard Do you know much about your husband's work?
Elsie No. I never had a mind for business.
Gerard Do you know if Sam had any enemies?
Elsie In business?
Gerard In anything.
Elsie None who would do this.
Gerard Have you ever heard of a man called Guy Haines?
Elsie Who's he?
Gerard An architect.
Elsie No.
Gerard His name doesn't ring any bells?
Elsie It might. My memory's always been bad, but lately ...
Gerard Has Charley ever mentioned him?
Elsie Not ... well ——
Gerard You never meant to hire him to build a house?

Elsie A house? No. Why would we build a house? We have a house. (*She thinks*) Wait ... No. I'm sorry. The headache hasn't quite gone away in all this time. It gets better, it gets worse, it gets better, it gets worse... but it doesn't ever quite go away.

Gerard His wife was murdered last June.

Elsie Whose?!

Gerard Guy Haines'.

Elsie Did he find her dead? Was he the one who found her?

Gerard (*with compassion*) No.

Elsie I found my husband. And I thank God for that! I can handle it. But Charley's fragile. It would have stayed with him forever. Thank God he's been spared that.

Gerard watches her in silence

He's very sensitive, you know — that's why he drinks. I had an uncle of the same temperament as Charley. He was a painter. He died young.

Gerard Mrs Bruno ...

She stands

Elsie I'll go take a nap now, if we're finished in here. My head is pounding.

Gerard If there's anything you need ...

Elsie (*freezing, looking out the window*) You know, there are worse things than what happened to us.

Gerard What do you mean?

Elsie I mean the thing itself is terrible — but there are worse things. What's worse, I find, for me, what's worse is that someone was watching all the time. Someone was looking at us. They could see us in the house. They could see us in our rooms.

Gerard I'm very sorry, Mrs Bruno.

Elsie I can't stop looking at the windows. I think someone's going to be there.

Elsie goes

The Lights cross-fade to the next scene

SCENE 5

The Haines's living-room

Anne enters from the kitchen with a plate of canapés

Anne (*calling off*) Oh, I've left my drink in there! Will you bring it in with you? (*She arranges canapés on the plate and sticks one in her mouth*)

Bruno enters with two drinks, puts one in front of her

Have one of these canapés while they're hot.

Bruno (*taking one*) You know, I wouldn't want to be anywhere else in the world tonight, Anne.

Anne How nice of you to say.

Bruno Thanks for letting me stay last night. I didn't expect such hospitality!

Anne I couldn't have sent you home in that state. Besides, it's nice to have a man in the house when Guy's away.

Bruno When I build my house, there's going to be a room in it just for you and Guy. It'll be your room! You can stay in it whenever you like.

Anne You're sweet. Where's your house going to be?

Bruno Not far from here. Just down the road in fact.

Anne It'll be nice to have a friend nearby.

Bruno Do you think Guy would like that?

Anne I'm sure he would. He's very fond of you, you know.

Bruno He is? Does he say that? There's *nothing* I wouldn't do for Guy! I love him like a brother.

Anne (*laughing*) Eat! They're for you.

Bruno Anne, do you think he'd build my house for me?

Anne I don't see why not. He built this one.

Bruno But this is where he lives. Do you think he'd build one for me?

Anne You can only ask. If he says no, I'll just have to work on him.

Bruno Would you do that?

Anne That's the fun of being a wife.

Bruno Oh, Anne, you don't know what that would mean to me! To live in a house *he built*! It's almost too much to imagine!

Anne (*offering canapés and sitting*) Have another.

Bruno You're one of the kindest, most generous women I've ever met. You can be my sister! Guy's my brother, and you're my sister! To my new family! (*He raises his glass*)

Anne laughs, lolls her head back against the couch, and shuts her eyes. Bruno stares at her neck. Long silence

You know, Guy must've found it hard, what happened to his wife and all that, but frankly, you're a much better wife to him than she was, aren't you? I mean, who wouldn't swap her for you any day?

She sits up. He indicates the bar

Can I ...

Anne Like I said, help yourself.

Bruno (*fixing himself a drink*) We've got to learn we have the power to make our lives better. People go on acting like they've got forever, but they haven't! Things like Miriam fit into our lives when we're living the sort of numb dream the rest of the world lives, but such things should be abandoned the minute we wake up from that dream, without sentiment, like that. (*He snaps his fingers*) Her loss is no loss to the world, that's for sure. (*He raises his glass, then drinks*)

Anne (*slightly shaken*) I didn't know you knew her.

Bruno I knew her. I mean, I never *met* her ... but I know her of old. They all deserve to get taught a thing or two, women like that — and women like you should dance on their graves, like this! (*He tries to dance*)

Anne Careful, you're going to fall!

Bruno I never fall! (*He stops dancing and moves in close to Anne*) I tell you, Anne, there's so much I could say to you if our spirits weren't suffocated by the *boring little facts of our existence*... but they are, so I can't. We just have to live with that. But one day, when time has passed, when we can hardly remember the childish thoughts we're thinking today, then maybe illusion won't be so dear to us and we can come to know each other at last. Ha!

Anne (*quietly*) Yes.

Bruno looks out the window

Bruno That's the aim of all great people. Was that a car? Does light go by when Guy comes home?

Silence. He drinks, staring out the window

Guy is everything to me. He represents everything, and he is everything. Everything that has the feeling of possibility in it, is Guy; everything else, is not. I want to know everything that's ever happened to him. I want to know every thought he's ever had, everything he's ever wanted, things he's forgotten he wanted. Every thought he's ever had should have been written down so none of it would have been lost. Before I die I'm going to go to Metcalf, which is a town I've never been to before... I'm going to go to this town, where Guy was born and grew up, where he lived and went to school and rode the merry-go-round and ate frozen custards and rowed boats, and while I'm there I'm going to pay my respects to his less fortunate wife at the place where she met her untimely end, ironically, if not downright comically, in the quiet dark of the Island of Love.

Guy comes in through the front door

Anne Darling, hallo.

Bruno Welcome home, Guy!

Anne Your friend Charles telephoned last night and came over with some more lovely flowers and it got so late I put him up in the spare room.

Bruno We've missed you, Guy. But we've had a great time together, haven't we Annie?

Anne (*to Guy*) Sweetie, let me get you a drink.

Bruno I'll do it.

Guy I don't want a drink.

Bruno Of course you do!

Guy You'll have to go now, Bruno. I'm tired and I'm ready for bed.

Bruno Oh now Guy ...

Anne He's waited all night and all day for you. Let's at least have a drink together.

Guy (*to Bruno*) You really will have to go.

Bruno Well it's too late now for me to get the train!

Guy (*moving to the phone*) I'll call you a taxi.

Anne But darling, it'll be so expensive!

Guy He can afford it.

Bruno Don't call just yet. (*He takes the phone out of Guy's hand*) Let me get you a drink, then after that you can make the call if you still want to. OK? What'll it be? Brandy?

Guy will not look at him

Anne (*to break the silence*) Yes. And one for me!

Bruno Two brandies and one Scotch on the rocks. (*He approaches the bar*) Oh, Annie, there's no ice!

Anne There's some in the freezer. I'll get it!

Anne exits through to the kitchen

Guy I want you to excuse yourself and go.

Bruno I have to tell you something!

Guy I don't want to hear it, *I want my home*!

Bruno You've got to hear it, Guy! Arthur Gerard's got your name. He's a private detective.

Guy turns to him, stunned

Don't look at me that way! He's not even a cop anymore. He's been working for my dad since I was a kid. Anyway, he's got it into his head he wants to find out what happened to my father. He's on his way here, but ——

Guy What?!

Bruno Would you relax? He's a thick-witted lump, and he's got nothing but your name!

Guy So what are you doing here? You want him to find you in our living-room?

Bruno I won't be down here, I'll be upstairs in the spare room, like last night!

Guy You're not going to stay here.

Bruno Please, Guy, please let me stay.

Guy No!

Bruno Just one more night!

Guy If you don't go I'll throw you out.

Bruno I will not go.

Guy moves toward Bruno

I'll tell! I'll tell her everything if you don't let me stay.

Guy stops

Why do I have to threaten you? Why can't you just let me stay because you *want* me to stay?

Guy Because I don't want you to stay. But stay if you have to. I feel nothing for you.

Bruno (*hurt*) Guy, stop saying things like that! God, I wish we could go to some other place where nobody knows us at all, some other planet even. This world is *so tiny* after what we've done... I feel like my life was all compressed into that one minute on the island in Metcalf when I was doing something *for you*, Guy, and now it seems like the rest of my life is just going to be chasing that moment again. I can't have it back! So, whether you want it or not, my life is yours. I have nowhere else to go.

Anne enters with a bowl of ice

Anne Ice.

Bruno Ice! (*He drops ice into his Scotch and gives them their brandies*) A brandy for you, and one for you. Now, what shall we toast?

Guy Nothing.

Bruno We've got to toast something! Anne, you choose! (*He clutches his belly in sudden pain*)

Anne Charles, what's wrong?

Bruno It's all right, it'll go in a second ...

Anne You'd better sit down.

Bruno I'll be fine. Think of a toast! I'm fine, see? (*He tries to stand up straight but clutches his belly again, bowing deeper than before*)

Anne Are you ill?
Bruno This happens at night sometimes, it really is nothing, I'll be fine if I just get a bit more Scotch in my belly ... (*He tries to drink*)

The doorbell rings

Anne Who on earth ——
Guy Wait. Don't answer it.
Bruno I'd better go upstairs.
Guy Take your glass!
Anne What's going on? Who's at the door?

Bruno grabs his glass and starts to go, but turns to Guy

Bruno Oh, we met at the Parker Institute in *December* ... didn't we, Guy?

Bruno ambles off

Anne Guy, tell me what's happening! Who's at the door?
Guy It's Arthur Gerard, a detective ——
Anne A detective!
Guy I'll explain it to you later, but for now, Bruno's not upstairs, all right?
Anne You want me to lie?
Guy Yes! For God's sake, *yes*!

Guy composes himself and opens the door

Gerard is there

Hallo.
Gerard Good-evening. I'm sorry to disturb you at this hour. I'm looking for a man called Guy Haines.
Guy I'm Guy Haines.
Gerard I'm Arthur Gerard, a private investigator.

He hands Guy his card

I'm afraid this is the closest thing we have to a badge in my business! Would you mind if I asked you a couple of questions?
Guy Not at all. Come in.

Gerard comes in and Guy closes the door behind him

This is my wife Anne.

Anne Hello. I'll leave you two alone.
Gerard No, please. If you don't mind, I'd like to talk to you both.
Guy Of course.
Anne Can I get you something to drink?
Gerard A Scotch with ice, if you have those things.
Anne We have Scotch, and we have ice.

She begins to fix Gerard a drink, as Guy gestures for Gerard to sit down

Gerard I welcome your hospitality.

The men sit

   You're an architect, aren't you, Mr Haines?
Guy Yes.
Gerard Did you build this house yourself?
Guy Yes.
Gerard Well in my humble opinion I think it's a beautiful house, though I
   don't profess to be an expert on such matters.
Anne We like it here, don't we Guy?
Gerard Do you build many houses, Mr Haines?

Anne turns to him with a drink

Anne None except ours — he's got a policy not to do houses for anybody
   else, which has been a bit of a bone of contention, since we had so many
   offers after the Palmyra. *He* had so many offers. Well, I can say "we", can't
   I? (*She giggles nervously*) Scotch on the rocks.

Gerard takes his drink, and Anne sits

Gerard Thank you. Do you know a man by the name of Charles Bruno?
Guy Yes, very slightly.
Gerard Did you meet through your work?
Guy Through my work ... ?
Gerard I mean as a result of your occupation as an architect. Forgive me if
   I'm unfamiliar with the terminology. Did he want you to build something
   for him?
Guy Oh! No. Not at all. We met at the Parker Art Institute, I think about last
   December. Yes, it was December, it was the Christmas party they give
   every year, where they invite all their old students, patrons, and other
   undesirables! Ha.
Gerard And what did you discuss?

Guy With Mr Bruno?

Gerard Yes.

Guy Oh, nothing, really! Nothing worth remembering. To tell you the truth, I can't remember much of what we discussed. I was rather the worse for wear.

Gerard If you don't remember what you said, perhaps you don't remember meeting Charles Bruno at that party. Maybe you met him at some other time. Or perhaps you do remember! I'm asking, not declaring.

Guy Oh, I remember meeting him. Who could forget meeting a man like that?

Gerard What was your ... unforgettable first impression of him?

Guy Well, I thought he was ... quite funny. Very bold, but he was drunk. He drank a lot! That was my main impression, he drank a lot, and he didn't have to go back to the bar because he kept refilling his glass from a little silver hip flask he had in his pocket which had grapes and apples engraved on it. He kept offering to fill my glass! Now I don't mind drinkers, I drink myself, as you can see, but that boy Bruno, he's heading for trouble, isn't he, he drinks like no-one I've ever seen!

Anne He even passed out at our wedding!

Gerard He went to your wedding?

Anne (*looking at Guy*) I believe he did, yes.

Gerard If you hardly know him, why did you invite him to your wedding?

Guy He just turned up.

Anne (*overlapping*) He called up, and asked if he could come. And I said yes.

Guy I didn't know that.

Anne He said he was a friend of yours.

Guy He's no friend of mine. Never was, never will be. Nope, that display at our wedding was enough for us, wasn't it, Anne? That was the last time we saw him, and the last time we intend to see him.

Gerard (*standing*) Well, I wouldn't be too hard on the boy. Maybe when he was at your wedding he wasn't his usual self.

Anne No?

Gerard Five days before your wedding someone got into the Bruno house through the back door, walked through the place like he knew it inside out, like he'd built it himself, climbed up the stairs to Charles' father's room, put a gun to his head, and sprayed the poor man all over the wall.

Anne Oh!

Gerard Sorry, Mrs Haines.

Anne (*to Guy*) Did you know that?

Guy No. I didn't know that.

Gerard Thank you for the drink.

Anne Stay for another if you like.

Guy No, honey, it's a long way back to Great Neck, I'm sure he wants to get on his way.

Gerard How did you know I've come from Great Neck?

Pause

Guy Your address was on your business card.
Gerard Oh! I'd forgotten.

Guy opens the door for him

Guy Can I ask you something?
Gerard Anything you like.
Guy Do you think Charles Bruno murdered his father?
Gerard No, son. He has an alibi. He was at the Palmyra.

Gerard nods and exits

Guy shuts the door behind him

Anne Guy, who is Charles Bruno? He's the man who wrote me that letter, isn't he. *Tell me!*
Guy Yes.
Anne Have you done something, Guy?
Guy Yes.
Anne Tell me what it is.
Guy I can't.
Anne Tell me!
Guy I'm afraid, Anne, I ——
Anne We're having a child. We're having a child. We're bound together more than you and Charles Bruno ever will be, so tell me what's happened — I know there's something, I've seen it in you, your eyes have gone cold — but maybe if I forgive you that'll be enough to help you *put an end to it for good*! Do you think it's something I'm not big enough to forgive you for? Well if it is, I'll just have to *get* big enough, because I live in the world, and in the world things happen, *big* things, and living *with* it, the whole *mess* of it — that's what makes it worth something. Isn't it? (*She begins to cry*) I'm willing, Guy. Let me try. And don't think I love you now or ever have loved you because you're good. I just love you because you're mine.
Guy I'll write it down. I'll write it down from start to finish, and give it to you, and it'll be out of me forever. (*He holds her*) You look at it. You see for me. I can't see.

He releases her and he goes through to the kitchen. She slowly moves off

The Lights cross-fade to the next scene

SCENE 6

Bruno's bedroom

Bruno enters, looking ill, feverishly searching for bottles. He finds one and drinks from it

Gerard appears in the doorway

Bruno Well look who's here. I thought we got lucky and you went back to Idaho.

Gerard smiles

Gerard Iowa. No I just went on a little trip.
Bruno Well why don't you go back on your trip, and stay there. As you can see I don't feel too well.

Gerard ignores this and moves into the room

Gerard I was looking for you on Friday night. No-one seems to know where you were.
Bruno What's it to you? I was at a friend's.
Gerard Which friend is that?
Bruno None of your business.
Gerard No?
Bruno It was Matt Levine, since it interests you so much.
Gerard Matt Levine is in custody on a fraud charge. I thought you knew that.
Bruno All right, I met a woman. I met a woman and I didn't want you to know about it because it's *none of your goddamn business*!
Gerard What was her name?

Silence

Was it Anne Haines?
Bruno I told you, I hardly know her.

Bruno drinks, but tentatively — he has trouble holding it down

Gerard I was there Friday night, at the home of Anne and Guy Haines. They gave me a drink. The reason I thought you might be there was because I asked for a Scotch on the rocks and she gave it to me without going into the kitchen for the ice. They were both drinking brandy, but there was a bowl of fresh ice on the bar.

Bruno (*trying to laugh*) They had fresh ice in the living-room, so that meant I was upstairs?

Gerard (*laughing with him*) No, that doesn't mean that at all.

Bruno You're some detective! Who taught you, Mickey Mouse?

Gerard No, it doesn't mean that at all. It can't mean that if you weren't upstairs!

Bruno Exactly.

Gerard But it got me thinking. If you *were* upstairs, why would you be there? And why would they say they hadn't seen you since the wedding? Why would they be hiding you? So I came to the conclusion that if you were upstairs, Guy Haines didn't want me to know you were friends.

Bruno You don't know anything. I'm getting out of here.

Gerard Oh no, Charley ——

Bruno *Don't call me Charley!* (*He turns on Gerard but falters, has to steady himself against the wall*)

Gerard You seem a bit shaky this morning.

Bruno You've got nothing on me. I know the road you're leading up, but you won't get anything on me because there's *nothing to get!*

Gerard Do you want to know what I was thinking?

Bruno *No!*

Gerard All right. I'll go.

Bruno *Go ahead then!* Tell me. You're wasting my time, but you might as well tell me now to get if off your chest.

Gerard Well, I asked Guy Haines what he thought of you when he first met you. He said he was impressed by how much you drank. He said when he met you at that party at the Parker Art Institute, you didn't bother with trips to the bar, you just filled up your glass from a silver hip flask you had in your possession which had grapes and apples engraved on it. Well I thought that was interesting because I remembered that flask, but I haven't seen if for a while. Not since December — or maybe even longer. So, when I arrived home Friday night I asked your mother when she saw it last. When I asked her that, it reminded her that she had it. She had your hip flask in her room. It was in a box on the corner table where she keeps cartons of sample perfume and half-opened mail. The box with the flask in it was posted to her from the Hotel La Fonda where you both stayed in Santa Fe. You left it in the room, so they mailed it to her. And she had it with her until Friday night, when she gave it to me to give to you. So here it is, Charles. You may have it.

Gerard takes the flask out of his coat pocket and hands it to Bruno

But then I thought, if Guy Haines remembers seeing this flask, and you haven't had it in your possession since June of last year, maybe he's a little mixed up. Maybe you met him earlier than December. I know you had the flask with you in June in Santa Fe, because that's where you left it, so perhaps he saw it in Santa Fe. He did go down to the Southwest about that time, but he couldn't have seen the flask in Santa Fe because he got off the train before then. He got off in Metcalf. So if he didn't see the flask in Santa Fe, where did he see it? Then it occurred to me that it was just possible that maybe he saw it on the train. Maybe you were on the same train together, travelling down to the great Southwest. I had the travel records checked and it seems I struck it lucky. You were on that train together. So I wondered if perhaps you met each other when you were on that train, and spoke to each other, and if that's maybe when he saw your hip flask.

Gerard's tone darkens

I decided to take a little trip myself, to see if I could fill in the picture and maybe find some of the people you met along the way. I was lucky there too. Any guesses? One of them was the waiter who served you both dinner on the train. He remembered you. You tipped him with a fifty. Another man remembered you as well, and that was the taxi driver who drove you from Magnolia Street in Metcalf Texas to Lake Metcalf's Kingdom of Fun, following a car with a red-haired girl in it. You didn't tip him at all. You were in too much of a hurry. The hotel books, phone bills, train records, and the testimony of a few kind gentlemen all seem to get you to Metcalf Texas for a twenty-four hour trip just in time for the previous Mrs Haines to get herself killed. (*Venomously*) But you know who I feel most sorry for, Charley? Guy Haines. I know malice when I see it and that boy is no murderer, not by a long stretch, so what you must've put him through to get him to kill your father I don't wish to imagine. How you must have told him he owed you, since you'd got him free. Free to start his life anew. Free to build beautiful things. But he was free of everything but the worst thing *not* to be free of in this world, and that is you, Charley Bruno. Charles.

Bruno's hand begins to shake, and he drops the bottle. He grabs his arm with his other hand, and his whole body buckles underneath him

Bruno Mother! (*He falls on to the floor and begins to jerk*) MOTH-ERRRRRRRRRR!

Elsie is just outside. She runs into the room

Elsie Darling, what's wrong?! Oh, help me Arthur, he's fallen!

Bruno I think I'm dying ...
Elsie He's shaking!
Gerard It's the DTs.
Bruno It's worse than the DTs. I'm dying ... Get me a drink!
Elsie OK, baby!
Bruno Hurry!

Elsie sees the bottle on the floor, grabs it, and begins to pour scotch into Bruno's mouth

Elsie Here you go, sweetie, drink this ... Drink ... this ...

Bruno guzzles and retches

Bruno Ma, look! Something's wrong with my hands!
Elsie I'll get a doctor!
Bruno *Don't let 'em take me away!* Lock all the doors!
Elsie They won't take you away, darling ——
Bruno *They will!* Don't call them and I won't drink again, I swear it with all my heart, mother, please!
Elsie Arthur, what should I do?!
Bruno Mother, my neck ... my lips ... I can't — speak ...
Elsie I won't let them touch you, baby, I won't let them take you away.

Bruno tries to speak but can't

Bruno (*sounds from deep within him*) Uhhhh ... Mahhhhh ...
Elsie I'll get you a wet cloth, baby. I'll be right back.

Elsie runs from the room

Bruno tries to breathe steadily, and succeeds in calming down

Gerard You're going to be all right. Trust me. I've seen people come back from farther out than where you are now. You won't be able to have another drink with even a drop of alcohol in it for the rest of your life or you'll die ... but other than that, you'll be fine. And I want you to know I'm off the case now. Guy Haines — if I'm right — has paid dearly for what he's done. He'll always be paying for it. And you, well ... you're not likely to do anything like that again, are you? So why should I have you sent to prison? The truth is ... you're already there.

Elsie runs in with a wet cloth, kneels beside Bruno, and mops his forehead

Elsie Here I am, baby. I'm back now. Mother's back.
Bruno Don't tell them it's the drink, Mother ...
Elsie I won't tell them, baby ...
Bruno I'll never touch it again.
Elsie Trust me, baby ... No-one's going to take you away.

Gerard moves to the door

Arthur, will you call the doctor on your way out?

Gerard nods assent and exits

They'll be here soon, baby ... You'll be OK now, just breathe deep and let me take care of everything ... (*She mops his forehead. She sees the Plato book on Bruno's dresser, stops mopping and stares at it for a moment, then resumes caressing him. It soon becomes apparent that she is holding back tears. She begins to sob*)
Bruno Mother, what's wrong? Mother?
Elsie Nothing...
Bruno Mother, how did you get here so quickly?
Elsie My baby ...
Bruno You heard him, didn't you. You were standing at the door.
Elsie I don't understand, baby ...
Bruno You heard ...
Elsie I don't know what he's saying ...
Bruno He's telling lies, Ma ... You didn't listen to it, did you?
Elsie I heard him. I head what he said.
Bruno He's a stupid man ...
Elsie I know — and I love my baby. So all the while he was talking I was thinking, my boy is telling the truth. He's a good boy, and he has no reason to lie ... But I just saw your book up there and it reminded me of something. I'm sorry, baby. I remembered ... (*She stands and goes to the Plato book on the dresser, lifts it up, and opens it, showing Bruno the inside cover*) Guy Haines. Metcalf, Texas. (*She breaks down crying*) What did you do, honey?
Bruno Nothing, Ma, I swear!
Elsie Baby, I'm scared.
Bruno Mother...
Elsie I don't understand everything. My mind is so tired lately. I don't remember any of this, don't worry... It would confuse me too much, so I don't remember any of it. But I can't be there for you any more, Charles.
Bruno Don't say that, Mother ...
Elsie You can't come to me ever again.

Bruno God, Ma, don't *say that*!

Elsie When you need to go to someone who knows you, baby, don't come
to me. I won't be there. (*She wipes her tears and looks at him distantly, as
though at a stranger*)

She walks to the door and leaves the room

Bruno Mother? *Mother, don't leave me alone!*

Bruno is reaching out toward the door, sobbing, but cannot get up

The Lights cross-fade to the next scene

SCENE 7

The Haines's living-room

Guy enters from the kitchen with a large envelope, sealed

Anne comes in from the other room and stands before him

He hands her the envelope and she takes it

*He clutches her tightly, then he goes out the front door. She takes the envelope
with her and goes off*

A dim blue light comes up downstage: the old railway yard

Guy comes in and looks around

After a time, Bruno appears

Bruno How do you like this old railway yard? It's where they put the trains
when they're no good any more. It's like a cemetery, a cemetery for trains.
Look, when the live trains pass it makes the dead ones light up and go out
again, light up and go out, like ghosts appearing and disappearing again in
the dark.

Guy This is the last time we'll be seeing each other.

Bruno Do you think this was ours, our train? It could have been ours.

Guy This is the last time.

Bruno I said that to you once before, and it didn't turn out to be true. People
say things that don't turn out to be true.

Guy This is true.

Bruno How can you be sure?

Guy Because I've told Anne.

Bruno Everything?

Guy I've written it down, from start to finish, from the time we met on the train...

Bruno This train!

Guy To this moment, to now. She knows where I am.

Bruno What did she say?

Guy She's reading it now. I left it with her.

Bruno I hope you explained it all the right way.

Guy What do you mean?

Bruno We told each other things we never told anybody else.

Guy She knows.

Bruno You liked me, did you tell her that? I didn't imagine that. Did you tell her that?

Guy Yes.

Bruno Because there's no point telling her unless you tell her the truth.

Guy is silent. He looks away

You know, there're not going to catch us now. Gerard was the only one who could've figured it out, and he's gone home now for good. Back to Iowa where he belongs! He was stupid, wasn't he? We outwitted them all, you and me!

Guy It doesn't matter to me now if we get caught or not. It's outside me now.

Bruno Of course it matters. That was the whole point!

Guy No. All that time, all those months I was left alone with it, with Miriam and then your father, left alone with those two, I was haunted by them. But when I wrote out the story for Anne it was like it was lifted out of me for good, not like it had never happened but like no matter what happens to you it's all right if you use it to make you free, not to cage you in, and now, now the police can come, they can put me in a cell and it would be just a detail, they could even take my life away from me and I would accept that with some grace, I know, because it's written down now, and it's out of me for good.

Bruno Let's go away somewhere. Just the three of us. I'll pay.

Guy You told me there was something you had to give me.

Bruno This.

Bruno takes out the revolver and sets it down between them

Guy I thought you were going to get rid of it.

Bruno But I had to be careful, Guy, somebody might've found it and then they could find you!

Guy They couldn't find me from that.

Bruno People must've seen you with it.

Guy It was a good luck charm. No-one knew I had it but me.

Bruno You're not going to let me build a house near you, are you?

Guy You can build a house wherever you want. You won't be welcome in mine.

Bruno Guy, please!

Guy Face the truth, Bruno! Face it and move on!

Bruno The truth, the truth, I've had a lot of truth to face! My mother's gone, I don't know where she went, she wouldn't tell me. She's just gone on a little trip, but she wouldn't tell me where. That's never happened before. I'm facing the truth of that. And the doctor says I can't drink any more — I mean, he's said it before, but now he says if I drink it's going to ruin my insides, and so I can't touch a drop, not a drop. There's the truth. I'm facing it. I'm facing all of it. (*He convulses with sobs*) What am I going to do?

Guy That's got nothing to do with me, Bruno.

Bruno Bruno?

Guy Charles...

Bruno "Charles"... Not even Charley. You hate the sound of it. (*He looks at Guy intensely*) You know, when I was alone with Anne there was a moment when she was on the couch, with her head back, and her neck was high and it was the lightest thing about her, her neck, and I thought, I could get even closer to Guy now. But then I thought, no-one could feel about me the way you feel about Anne, or the way Anne feels about you. You can't kill that fact.

Guy turns and begins to walk away. Bruno takes out the Plato book and reads from it. Guy freezes when he hears him

"This is love, O Socrates, for the sake of which all the former labours were endured. It is pure, eternal, indestructible. It does not grow or die. It is whole and unchanging forever, and all that is beautiful is beautiful because of it. O Socrates, this is the truth I speak: that whosoever should gaze upon it in this life abandons his soul to the everlasting. He becomes dear to the gods, and, if such a privilege is given to any human being, he is made, himself, immortal."

Guy turns and looks at him. Bruno picks up the gun

I thought I'd be immortal but I haven't even had mortality. I had one minute's life on an island in Metcalf when I was really somewhere, doing something — and the minute's over.

Bruno puts the barrel to his own chest

Guy Please don't do that…
Bruno What do you care?
Guy There were no bullets left!
Bruno Then I'll live won't I?
Guy Please, Bruno…
Bruno Bruno? I have to do it now, Guy … You know why?
Guy Why…?
Bruno Because you didn't call me by my first name.

Bruno shoots himself in the heart and collapses dead. Guy falls to his knees beside Bruno and sobs

After a time, Anne appears beside him

Anne Guy!
Guy He's dead …
Anne Don't look at him. You don't know him.
Guy Anne…
Anne Stand up.
Guy We can't leave him there…
Anne You've given him enough. Take my hand.
Guy But what'll I do now, Anne? *What I'll do?*
Anne I've read your story. I've burned it now and it's gone.
Guy You can't burn it though, you can't just burn it …
Anne If you stay here now you'll be found with him and it'll never be over.
    Come with me. Your friend called again.
Guy My friend?
Anne You've got work to do, Guy. He wants you to build a bridge.

She reaches her hand out to him. Guy looks at Bruno, then up at Anne. He lifts himself up, grabs the Plato book, takes Anne's hand and she leads him off

The lighting changes to suggest, faintly, a bridge in beams and columns of white light. Anne and Guy run across up stage, as——

——the CURTAIN *falls*

FURNITURE AND PROPERTY LIST

Only essential items have been listed. Further dressing may be added at the director's discretion, as facilities permit. Please see the Author's Note on page vi concerning the staging of the original production.

Please see the note on page 72 concerning the use of firearms.

ACT I

SCENE 1

	DINING-CAR
On stage:	Seats
	Table. *On it*: glass for **Guy,** copy of Plato for **Guy**
Off stage:	Glass containing Scotch (Bruno)
Personal:	**Bruno**: wrist-watch (worn throughout), silver hip flask containing Scotch

SCENE 2

	HOTEL ROOM
On stage:	Dressing-table with mirror. *On table*: various items of make-up, copy of Plato book, phone
	Chair
Off stage:	Glass of scotch (**Bruno**)
Personal:	**Bruno**: silver hip flask containing scotch

SCENE 3

	VILLA IN MEXICO
On stage:	Table. *On it*: phone

SCENE 4

	NEW YORK BAR
On stage:	Table
	4 chairs

| *Off stage*: | 2 drinks (**Bruno**) |
| | Alligator briefcase (**Guy**) |

Personal: **Bruno**: initialled tie in pocket

SCENE 5

	HAINES'S LIVING-ROOM
On stage:	Fireplace
	Window open

SCENE 6

	GUY'S ROOM
On stage:	Bed. *On it*: bedclothes, letter and envelope for **Guy**
	Guy's coat
	Bedside table. *In drawer*: gun
	Bureau. *In drawers*: bundles of letters and envelopes. *On it*: candle.
	Above it: mirror
	Metal wastebasket
	Cooker (practical)
	Kettle with water
	Cups, saucers, etc.
	Kitchenette curtain closed

Off stage: Pencil, paper (**Bruno**)

SCENE 7

	GUY'S OFFICE AND THE STREET OUTSIDE
On stage:	Desk. *On it*: phone
	Table
	2 chairs
	Pubic phone in street

Off stage: Large envelope containing folded, large drawing (**Stage Management**)

SCENE 8

| | GUY'S ROOM |
| *On stage*: | As before |

| *Set*: | Old sketchbooks on bed |
| | Notebook on dresser |

Re-set: Kitchenette curtain half-closed

Personal: **Guy**: doorkeys
                 Anne: letter and envelope in pocket

SCENE 9

                 BRUNO'S BEDROOM
On stage: Bed. *On it*: bedclothes, almost full overnight bag. *Under mattress*:
                     Plato book
                 Dresser
                 Photographs on wall
                 Concealed bottles, 1 containing Scotch, the rest empty

SCENE 10

                 HAINES'S LIVING-ROOM
On stage: As before

Set: Couch
                 Coffee-table. *On it*: phone

                 GUY'S ROOM
Set: kitchenette curtain closed

Off stage: Overnight bags (**Anne**)

Personal: **Guy**: lighter

ACT II
SCENE 1

                 HAINES'S LIVING-ROOM
On stage: As before

Set: Bar. *On it*: various bottles of drink, including Scotch and brandy,
                     glasses

Off stage: Camera with practical flash (**Myers**)
                 Drink (**Bruno**)

Personal: **Myers**: spare film
                 Bruno: revolver in pocket

SCENE 2

GERARD'S OFFICE
On stage: Desk. *On it*: ashtray
                  2 chairs

SCENE 3

HAINES'S LIVING-ROOM
On stage: As before

Off stage: Vase of exotic flowers (**Anne**)

SCENE 4

GERARD'S OFFICE
On stage: As before

Personal: **Elsie**: lighted cigarette

SCENE 5

HAINES'S LIVING-ROOM
On stage: As before

Off stage: Plate of canapés (**Anne**)
                  2 drinks (**Bruno**)
                  Bowl of ice (**Anne**)

Personal: **Gerard**: business card

SCENE 6

BRUNO'S BEDROOM
On stage: As before

Re-set: Plato book on dresser

Off stage: Wet cloth (**Elsie**)

Personal: **Gerard**: **Bruno**'s silver hip flask in pocket

SCENE 7

	HAINES'S LIVING-ROOM
On stage:	As before
Off stage:	Large sealed envelope (**Guy**)
Personal:	**Bruno**: revolver in pocket

LIGHTING PLOT

Property fittings required: nil

Various interior and exterior settings

ACT I

To open: General interior lighting on dining-car area

Cue 1	**Bruno**: "Please call me Charley." *Cross-fade to hotel room for Scene 2*	(Page 7)
Cue 2	**Bruno** goes into the bathroom *Cross-fade to villa room for Scene 3*	(Page 9)
Cue 3	**Anne** reaches out and touches **Guy**'s cheek *Cross-fade to bar area* DR *for Scene 4*	(Page 12)
Cue 4	**Bruno** finishes **Guy**'s drink *Cross-fade to* **Haines**'s *living-room for Scene 5*	(Page 16)
Cue 5	**Guy**: "I don't want any surprises." *Cross-fade to stairs* R *for Scene 6*	(Page 19)
Cue 6	**Bruno**: "... will be just on your right." *Bring up dim lighting on* **Guy**'s *room*	(Page 20)
Cue 7	**Bruno** exits *Fade lighting on stairs* R	(Page 21)
Cue 8	**Guy** turns out the lights *Black-out*	(Page 21)
Cue 9	To open Scene 7 *Bring up lighting on* **Guy**'s *office and public telephone in street*	(Page 21)
Cue 10	**Myers** puts the phone down *Fade lighting on street*	(Page 22)

Cue 11   **Bruno** appears DL   (Page 22)
           Bring up lighting on **Bruno**

Cue 12   **Guy** goes out the door   (Page 23)
           Fade lighting on office; bring up lighting on street area
              downstage

Cue 13   **Bruno**: "... about Anne Faulkner?"   (Page 24)
           Bring up gentle light on **Guy**'s *room*

Cue 14   **Bruno** and **Guy** exit   (Page 25)
           Fade lighting on street area downstage; increase lighting
              in **Guy**'s *room*

Cue 15   **Anne**: " '... to his bedroom to sleep.' "   (Page 25)
           Bring up dim lighting on stairs R

Cue 16   **Guy** jerks himself back to reality   (Page 26)
           Snap off lighting on stairs R

Cue 17   **Guy** turns off the lights   (Page 27)
           Reduce to very dim level in **Guy**'s *room*

Cue 18   **Guy** goes out   (Page 27)
           Cross-fade to **Bruno**'s *bedroom for Scene 9*

Cue 19   **Bruno** exits with his bag   (Page 29)
           Cross-fade to **Haines**'s *living-room for Scene 10*

Cue 20   **Anne** goes to the phone and dials   (Page 29)
           Bring up very dim lighting in **Guy**'s *room*

Cue 21   **Anne** sits on the couch   (Page 29)
           Fade lighting in **Haines**'s *living-room*

Cue 22   **Guy** lights a candle   (Page 30)
           Bring up covering spot in **Guy**'s *room*

Cue 23   **Guy** stares at his face in the mirror   (Page 31)
           Bring up gentle light in **Bruno**'s *bedroom and lighting*
              on **Haines**'s *living-room*

Cue 24   **Elsie** switches off the light   (Page 31)
           Snap off lighting in **Bruno**'s *bedroom*

Cue 25   **Guy** blows out the candle   (Page 31)
           Snap off lighting in **Guy**'s *room*

Cue 26	**Anne** turns off the lights *Snap off lighting*	(Page 32)
Cue 27	**Bruno** exits *Bring up dim lighting on stairs* R	(Page 32)

ACT II

To open: General interior lighting on the **Haines**'s living-room

Cue 28	**Anne** leads **Guy** out *Cross-fade to **Gerard**'s office for Scene 2*	(Page 40)
Cue 29	**Bruno** exits *Cross-fade to the **Haines**'s living-room for Scene 3*	(Page 42)
Cue 30	**Guy** exits *Cross-fade to **Gerard**'s office for Scene 4*	(Page 44)
Cue 31	**Elsie** goes *Cross-fade to the **Haines**'s living-room for Scene 5*	(Page 45)
Cue 32	**Guy** and **Anne** exit *Cross-fade to **Bruno**'s bedroom for Scene 6*	(Page 54)
Cue 33	**Bruno** reaches out toward the door, sobbing *Cross-fade to the **Haines**'s living-room for Scene 7*	(Page 59)
Cue 34	**Anne** goes off *Cross-fade to dim blue light downstage*	(Page 59)
Cue 35	**Anne** leads **Guy** off *Cross-fade to faintly suggest a bridge in beams and columns of white light*	(Page 62)

EFFECTS PLOT

ACT I

ACT II

FIREARMS (AMENDMENT) BILL

Samuel French is grateful to Charles Vance, Vice-Chairman of the Theatres Advisory Council, for the following information regarding the Firearms (Amendment) Bill:

"The Firearms (Amendment) Bill does not affect blank-firing pistols which are not readily convertible (i.e. those which do not require a Firearms Certificate). Among the reasons against imposing restrictions on such items is their use in theatre, cinema and television as a 'safe' alternative to real guns.

The general prohibition on the possession of real handguns will apply to those used for theatrical purposes. It would clearly be anomalous to prohibit the use of those items for target shooting, but permit their use for purposes where a fully-working gun is not needed. As handguns will become 'Section 5' prohibited weapons, they would fall under the same arrangements as at present apply to real machine guns. As you will know, there are companies which are authorised by the Secretary of State to supply such weapons for theatrical purposes.

The exemption under Section 12 of the Firearms Act 1968, whereby actors can use firearms without themselves having a Firearms Certificate, will remain in force".

Regulations apply to the United Kingdom only. Producers in other countries should refer to appropriate legislation.

Lightning Source UK Ltd.
Milton Keynes UK
UKOW01f0052010218
317161UK00005B/124/P

9 780573 019722